Americans of Dream and Deed (Second Edition)

(A READING SKILLS TEXT)

Lila Lowenherz
Robert J. Lowenherz

When ordering this book, please specify
either **R 581 S** *or* AMERICANS OF DREAM AND DEED,
SECOND EDITION

AMSCO SCHOOL PUBLICATIONS, INC.
315 Hudson Street   New York, N.Y. 10013

Acknowledgments

Grateful acknowledgment is made to the following sources for permission to use copyrighted and other materials, which appear on the pages indicated.

CBS Inc.: 107–108, quotation from the CBS Evening News, © 1966

The photographs were supplied through the courtesy of:

The Bettmann Archive, Inc.: 17, 41, 62, 99, 106, 119, 133, 176, 218, 221
Culver Pictures, Inc.: 26, 183
FPG: 126, 159
June Harrison/Photographer: facing page 1
The Library of Congress: 55, 234
Mark Twain Memorial, Hartford, CT: 203
United States Olympic Committee: 140

Cover by Ted Bernstein

ISBN 1-56765-004-X
NYC Item 56765-004-9

4   5   6   7   8   9   10   00   99

To the Student

The great American writer Mark Twain once said that the story of a person's life is like the moon. We always see the same shining white face of the moon turned toward us. But there is another side of the moon, which remains dark and hidden from our sight. So it is with a person's life.

In *Americans of Dream and Deed*, you will see both sides of the lives of 19 famous men and women. You will read the stories of their bold and shining dreams, and the ways they made those dreams come true. But you will also learn something about the doubts and fears and troubles—the "other side of the moon"—in their lives.

This personal, human side of each life will help you understand better the men and women in the stories. It will also make each story meaningful and interesting. You will see that almost all these honored people had to overcome some of the same doubts and fears and problems that you face in your own life.

The people whose stories are told in this book may seem very different from one another. Some are rich, while others are terribly poor. They come from different races, religions, and ways of life. As you read their stories, though, you will see that these people are alike in one important way. They do not ask of life, "What's in it for me?" Instead, they ask, "What is in me that I can give to life? How can I help make the lives of other people better and happier?"

Perhaps you have asked yourself these same or similar questions and wondered about the answers. Reading this book may help you discover answers to your questions. It's up to you to choose a course of life that feels right for you. When you do, you too may become an American of dream and deed.

Lila Lowenherz
Robert J. Lowenherz

iii

To the Teacher

Americans of Dream and Deed: A Reading Skills Text offers 18 original biographies of outstanding American men and women whose lives range broadly from colonial times to the present. These men and women reflect the ethnic, religious, and cultural pluralism of America. The stories of their lives provide variety, conflict, and drama, affording high interest for the student. Although easy to read, the stories are nevertheless mature in content, historically accurate, and biographically sound.

The authors have imbued the text with certain ethical values: social concern and involvement; a belief in the dignity of the individual; and a faith in the strength and integrity of America and in the old-fashioned virtues of plain living, bold dreaming, and hard work. We chose to write about the individuals in this text because they exemplify these values and because their lives are adventurous and interesting.

Americans of Dream and Deed uses the biographies as the basis for developing students' reading, writing, speaking, listening, and thinking skills as follows:

1. Brief sets of exercises, after every page or two of the text of each biography, promote active reading. Picking up a pen or pencil, students immediately become involved in locating details, recalling facts, determining main ideas, and working with vocabulary in the text. With these relatively easy exercises, students begin to build their reading skills and their self-confidence.

2. Abundant and varied sets of exercises at the end of each biography further develop reading and thinking skills. These exercises consist of: putting events in sequence, making inferences, understanding cause and effect, separating fact from opinion, and choosing the best title. Two final sets of exercises offer activities and topics for speaking, listening, and brief writing assignments.

We hope that *Americans of Dream and Deed* will provide students with a pleasurable reading experience as well as an opportunity to learn about the lives of some distinguished American men and women. We trust, too, that the exercises in this text will help students develop the self-confidence that comes from their mastery of reading and other essential communication skills.

The Authors

Contents

Americans of Dream and Deed

A top woman tennis star plays to win more than tennis games.

1. *Billie Jean King*

Part I

1   **On September 20, 1973,** a tennis court was set up in the Astrodome, the huge stadium in Houston, Texas. The largest crowd that ever watched a tennis match gathered there. Millions of fans in 37 countries viewed the game on TV. For this was no ordinary tennis match. The newspapers called it the "Battle of the Sexes."

2   Billie Jean King, then 29, was the best woman player of that time. She faced Bobby Riggs, a man of 55. Years before, he had ranked among the world's greatest tennis stars. Even at 55, he was still a strong player.

3   Bobby Riggs had a low opinion of women tennis players. He believed that women are not the equal of men and dared any of the top female players to beat him. He pointed proudly to his recent victory over Margaret Smith Court, the Australian star. Now he was out to beat Billie Jean.

4   "If any woman wants to spend an hour and a half of her time proving women are as good as men," he boasted to reporters, "now's her chance."

5   "I tell you," he said to Billie Jean, "you not only cannot beat a top male player, but you can't beat me, a tired old man."

6   Billie Jean was quick to accept the challenge, and a five-set match was arranged. To win a match of five sets,

1

she would have to win at least 18 games. Such a long match favored her because she was young, strong, and fast on her feet.

7   From the moment Billie Jean served the first ball, Bobby Riggs was in trouble. She made him run after the ball from one side of the court to the other. Before long, his clothes were soaked with sweat. The young woman won set after set. At last, the match was hers. After scoring the last point, Billie Jean threw her racket into the air for joy.

8   "I didn't win this match for myself," she told reporters. "I did it for women's tennis."

Finding Details

To be a good reader, you don't have to remember every detail or fact you read. You must be able to find important details, however, by skimming, or reading very quickly, what you have already read. The following exercises will help you develop this skill.

(*Note*: For easy reference, each paragraph is numbered in the margin. *Write your answers to all exercises on a separate sheet of paper.*)

1. Give the number of the paragraph in which you learn the answer to each of the following questions.
   a. When did the "Battle of the Sexes" take place?
   b. At the time of the match, how old were Bobby Riggs and Billie Jean?
   c. What did Bobby Riggs say to Billie Jean?
   d. How many sets had to be played in the match?

2. The number of the paragraph that tells how Bobby Riggs felt about female tennis players is:
   (*a*) 1   (*b*) 2   (*c*) 3   (*d*) 4

Part II

9 **At her first tournament,** Billie Jean, then 12 years old, learned that men made the rules for female tennis players. As pictures were being taken of the players, Perry Jones, the president of the Southern California Tennis Association, suddenly pointed at her.

10 "Not you," he said. "You can't be in the picture because you aren't dressed properly."

11 "I was wearing a blouse and a nice pair of white tennis shorts my mother had made for me," Billie Jean remembered. "But Jones had this rule: Boys wore shorts and girls wore dresses, and that was that. I found out," she added, "that these people were more concerned with what you wore than how you played. I also found out that men were making the decisions about what women should do."

12 Billie Jean was determined to make her own decisions. A year earlier, she had told her mother, "I'm going to be the best tennis player in the world." To make that dream come true, she practiced endlessly under the hot California sun to perfect her game. With good coaching and hard work, she became a fine player. At 17, she was ranked the fourth best American player in amateur women's tennis.

13 Then came Wimbledon! Every good tennis player dreams of competing at Wimbledon, England, because the most important tournaments in the world are played there. At these tournaments, players from many countries compete against each other. The winners then play to see who is best.

14 Billie Jean had played at Wimbledon before, but she hadn't done very well. In 1966, however, she was serious. She was out to win, and she did! For the first time in her career, she beat the best women players to win the singles title. Billie Jean King was now the top female tennis player in the world.

Writing Details

3. In this part of the story, you learned more details about Billie Jean King. On a separate sheet of paper, write the missing details in each of the following sentences.
   a. Billie Jean learned that men made the _____ for female tennis players.
   b. People were more concerned with what you _____ than how you played.
   c. Billie Jean could not have her picture taken because she was wearing _____.

4. How skilled are you at picking out details in what you read? Write how old Billie Jean was when she:
   a. played in her first tournament
   b. said, "I'm going to be the best tennis player in the world." (*Hint*: You have to figure out this one.)
   c. was ranked as the fourth best amateur women's tennis player

Part III

15   **Making it to the top** in sports is never easy. Staying there is even harder. Besides, Billie Jean had other problems.

16   Beginning in 1968, she had to have three operations on her knee. After each operation, she exercised for months to strengthen her legs. Billie Jean was not going to let problems with her knee slow her down or interfere with her tennis game.

17   She had money problems, too. So she became a tennis pro, or professional, to be able to earn money from the sport. In pro tennis, however, women were not well paid. Men earned five times as much as women did. An angry Billie Jean decided to do something about this unfair treatment.

18   In the late 1960s and early 1970s, she led a group of the best women tennis players on a special tour around the country. In city after city, the group drew large crowds and substantial profits. In 1971, she became the first woman player to make more than $100,000 in one year. Because of the tour and Billie Jean's success, other women were also able to earn more money by playing tennis.

19   A National Women's Conference in 1977 brought thousands of women to the Astrodome in Texas—including Billie Jean. Four years earlier, she had beaten Bobby Riggs there, and now she was back in the same stadium, still fighting to win respect and more money for women tennis players.

20   Billie Jean went on working for women's rights and playing great tennis. During the 1970s and 1980s, she set up team-tennis leagues all over the United States. In team tennis, women play not only against other women, but also against men. As a solo player, Billie Jean was still in top form. In 1979, she won her 20th title at Wimbledon.

21   Through the 1980s, she worked even harder to develop team-tennis leagues all over the nation. Why was this work so important to her?

22   "Boys and girls need to be playing on the same teams together," she explained. "I promised myself when I finished playing I'd work on team tennis. This will be my biggest contribution."

23   As her other contribution to tennis, she helps train younger players. She tries to improve both their game and their attitudes as players. In 1990, for example, she gave lessons to a promising new tennis star. When they played doubles together for the first time, Billie Jean King, age 46, and Jennifer Capriati, age 13, both won.

24   "I believe that if you really want something, you should go for it," Billie Jean once told a group of young people. "You'll never know if you can get it unless you try."

Finding the Main Idea

Have you ever listened to someone ramble on from one detail to another to another? After a while, you probably felt like saying, "Would you please get to the point!" A good speaker or writer ties together the details and makes them meaningful by telling you the point, or main idea, of those details. As a good reader, you must be able to identify the main idea of a paragraph or even a group of paragraphs.

5. The main idea of paragraph 18 is best expressed by sentence:
   (*a*) 1   (*b*) 2   (*c*) 3   (*d*) 4

6. The main idea of paragraph 20 is best expressed by sentence:
   (*a*) 1   (*b*) 2   (*c*) 4   (*d*) 5

Working with Words

To make the most sense of what you read, you must constantly sharpen your word power. In the following exercises, you will strengthen your skill with words.

7. *Boasted* (paragraph 4) means:
   (*a*) shouted   (*b*) explained   (*c*) asked   (*d*) bragged

8. An *amateur* (paragraph 12) does something for:
   (*a*) money   (*b*) revenge   (*c*) pleasure   (*d*) duty

9. The phrase closest in meaning to *competing* (paragraph 13) is:
   (*a*) helping others   (*b*) finishing early
   (*c*) trying to win   (*d*) improving one's game

10. A person on a *tour* (paragraph 18) would most likely:
   (*a*) travel   (*b*) talk   (*c*) attend classes   (*d*) eat at home

EXERCISES

Putting Events in Sequence

In reading the story of a person's life—or any story—you know that events follow each other in some kind of order, or sequence. Remembering the order of events helps you get a clearer picture of what you read.

A.   Write the letters of each set of events in the order in which the events happened in Billie Jean's life. For example, would you answer #1 by writing *a-b* or *b-a*? If you need help, look back at the story.

1. *a.* Bobby Riggs beats Margaret Smith Court.
   b. Billie Jean plays against Bobby Riggs in the Houston Astrodome.

2. *a.* She is ranked as the fourth best American player in amateur women's tennis.
   b. She plays in her first tournament.

3. *a.* She wins the singles title at Wimbledon for the first time.
   b. Perry Jones does not allow her to be photographed.

4. *a.* She sets up team-tennis leagues.
   b. She has to have knee operations.

5. *a.* She returns to the Houston Astrodome for a women's rights conference.
   b. She becomes a tennis pro.

Making Inferences

A detective has to figure out what certain clues mean. As a reader, you can use clues to draw conclusions from what you have read. When you "read between the lines" in this way, you are making inferences.

Example: Billie Jean came from:
(*a*) New York   (*b*) London   (*c*) Florida   (*d*) California

Explanation: Although you are never told directly where Billie Jean was born and raised, clues from Part II, paragraphs 9 and 12, help you to infer that the correct choice is (*d*) California.

B.   Use what you have read about Billie Jean King to infer, or figure out, the correct choice.

1. Bobby Riggs' poor opinion of women tennis players was most likely shared by:
   (*a*) Billie Jean   (*b*) Billie Jean's mother
   (*c*) Perry Jones   (*d*) Margaret Smith Court

2. An amateur tennis player is *not* allowed to:
   (*a*) compete at Wimbledon   (*b*) play abroad
   (*c*) play for money   (*d*) wear shorts

3. The Bobby Riggs–Billie Jean King match was played in the Houston Astrodome because of its:
   (*a*) fame   (*b*) location   (*c*) inexpensiveness   (*d*) size

4. With which of the following statements would Billie Jean be most likely to agree?
   (*a*) A woman's place is in the home.
   (*b*) Women and men should have equal opportunities.
   (*c*) Men are naturally superior to women.
   (*d*) Women are naturally superior to men.

Understanding Cause and Effect

Whenever you ask *why* something happened, you are asking about cause and effect. By understanding cause and effect as you read, you will see important connections between two or more facts or events.

Example: Billie Jean was able to win the singles title at Wimbledon in 1966 partly because of her:
(*a*) youth   (*b*) experience at team tennis
(*c*) defeat of Bobby Riggs   (*d*) determination

Explanation: A cause must come before an effect, or result. Since choices (*b*) and (*c*) refer to events after 1966, those events cannot be causes. Part II, paragraph 14, tells you that she "had played at Wimbledon before, but she hadn't done very well." Since her youth had not helped her in the past, choice (*a*) can be ruled out. Paragraph 14 also tells you that "she was serious" and "out to win." Thus, she had determination, and choice (*d*) is correct.

C.   Write the letter of the best choice.

1. Billie Jean became a tennis pro because she:
   (*a*) won at Wimbledon   (*b*) had knee operations
   (*c*) needed money   (*d*) wanted to play team tennis

2. Which of the following made Billie Jean fight for women's rights?
   (*a*) She needed knee operations.
   (*b*) In pro tennis, men earned five times as much as women did.
   (*c*) She earned more than $100,000 in one year.
   (*d*) She won the women's singles title at Wimbledon in 1966.

3. Bobby Riggs challenged Billie Jean to play against him because of all women players she was then the:
   (*a*) youngest   (*b*) oldest   (*c*) best   (*d*) least experienced

4. As a result of Billie Jean's work, other women players could:
   (*a*) become tennis pros   (*b*) win at Wimbledon
   (*c*) earn more money   (*d*) go on tour

Separating Fact from Opinion

Both in reading and in your daily life, it is often important for you to be able to tell the difference between a fact and an opinion. A fact can be checked out to determine if it is true. An opinion shows how someone feels or thinks about something, and cannot be checked out to see if it is true or false. For example, "It is 20 degrees outdoors" is a fact. "It is too cold for comfort" is an opinion.

D.   Tell which is a *fact* and which is an *opinion.*

1. Women tennis players should not compete against men play-ers.

2. Billie Jean attended a National Women's Conference in 1977.

3. Bobby Riggs was 55 when he played Billie Jean.

4. Women tennis players ought to earn as much money as men players do.

Choosing the Best Title

You have found the main idea of a paragraph. Now you must find the main idea of a much larger piece of writing. In this more challenging kind of question, the main idea is given in the form of a title. By choosing the best title, you show that you understand the main idea of the entire story of Billie Jean King.

E.   Write the number of the best title for the story of Billie Jean.

1. Billie Jean King Defeats Bobby Riggs

2. How to Play Tennis

3. Champion of Sportswomen

4. Women in Tennis

Speaking, Listening, and Writing

Reading is only one way that you communicate, or exchange facts and feelings with others. Speaking, listening, and writing are also important ways of communicating. Many of the skills you use when you read serve equally well when you speak, listen, or write. In the following activities, you will have a chance to develop your skills in these other forms of communication.

F.   Listen while two or more of your classmates debate, or take sides on, one of the following topics. Be prepared to tell which side you think made the better argument—and why. (*Hint:* It may help if you take notes while you listen.)

1. Do you think that women can compete with men in some sports?

2. Billie Jean believes that most men do not like being beaten in sports by women. Do you agree or disagree with her opinion? Tell why.

G.   Write a paragraph or more about one of the following topics.

1. Why was the tennis match between Bobby Riggs and Billie Jean important?

2. What are some of the things Billie Jean did to help improve women's tennis?

3. How do you think Billie Jean feels about girls' playing Little League baseball? Explain your answer.

A young lawyer takes on big business and big government to protect the American consumer.

2. Ralph Nader

Part I

1   **"I think I'm being followed,"** Ralph Nader told his friends.

2   "Don't be silly," they said. "You must be imagining things."

3   "Strange people are calling me up in the middle of the night," he went on. "One of them said, 'Why don't you go back to Connecticut, buddy boy?' "

4   What was this all about?

5   Until 1965, Ralph Nader had been a young, unknown lawyer from Connecticut. Then he wrote *Unsafe at Any Speed*, a book about automobile safety in which he claimed that the automobile companies cared more about making money than making safe cars.

6   The strongest attack in his book was against a General Motors compact car, the Corvair. Its poor design, he wrote, made the Corvair a death trap.

7   He demanded a law giving the United States government the power to set safety standards for automobiles. As you can guess, the automobile makers did not want any such law.

8   Ralph Nader might have remained an unknown lawyer from Connecticut if General Motors had not made a big mistake. The company hired a detective agency to find out about him.

9   Detectives visited people who knew him and asked all kinds of questions: "What sort of guy is he? Does he drink? Does he use drugs? Who are his friends? Where does he get his money? Why does he care about auto safety?"

10   One day the whole secret operation against Ralph Nader blew up. He was visiting Washington, D.C., to talk to a group of United States senators who were working on the first national automobile safety law. Two private detectives were caught trying to follow him into the offices of the United States Senate. When the story came out in the newspapers, General Motors was forced to admit that it had hired the detectives.

11   The president of General Motors was ordered to appear before the group of senators. On one side of the room sat the head of one of the richest and most powerful companies in America. On the other side of the room sat Ralph Nader.

12   Then the people of America heard the full story of the attempt to smear Ralph Nader. They heard the president of General Motors say, "I want to apologize here and now to Mr. Nader."

13   A few months later, the United States Senate passed the National Traffic and Motor Vehicle Safety Act. It was the law Ralph Nader had worked for.

14   The General Motors case helped make him known all over America. Ralph Nader, the private citizen, became Mr. Public Citizen.

Finding Details

1. Give the number of the paragraph in which Ralph Nader:
   a. said he was being followed
   b. wrote a book
   c. criticized the Corvair
   d. visited Washington, D.C.

2. The number of the paragraph in which detectives asked people about Ralph Nader is:
(*a*) 3   (*b*) 9   (*c*) 12   (*d*) 14

Part II

15   **Ralph Nader cares deeply** about the rights and well-
being of others. That caring began with his family and
childhood.

16   His father and mother, Nathra and Rose Nader,
were born in the Middle Eastern nation of Lebanon.
Like many other people who came to live in America,
Nathra and Rose arrived with only a few dollars. They
worked hard and saved their money.

17   In time, the family moved to the town of Winsted in
northern Connecticut. There Nathra and Rose bought a
house and also opened a restaurant called the Highland
Arms.

18   The Naders had four children, two girls and two
boys. The youngest child, born in 1934, was Ralph.

19   It was not just being Lebanese that made Nathra and
Rose Nader different from their neighbors. They would
have stood out anywhere, anytime. Both of them had
strong opinions. They were interested in new ideas and
new ways of doing things. Above all, they believed, as
Nathra used to say, that citizens must give more to their
country than they take from it.

20   In this spirit, the Naders were very active in Winsted.
They went to all the town meetings and spoke up for
their beliefs. They worked hard on everything they
thought was good for the town—from new sewers to a
new community college.

21   Both in the Highland Arms Restaurant and at home, the talk flowed without end. Nathra liked to discuss the workings of big business and the government, and the problems of the American people.

22   During supper time at home, the family and even visitors used to play a game that Nathra made up. He called it "What if . . . ?"

23   "What if you were President of the United States and millions of Americans couldn't find jobs? What would you do?"

24   "What if you found out that the company you worked for did something dishonest, but if you said anything, you would lose your job? What would you do?"

25   Each person at the table tried to come up with an answer. Everybody learned something from the game because it made them all think about things in a new way.

26   Nathra and Rose also believed strongly in the value of learning. When Ralph was a child, his mother once pointed to his head. "You have a very good storage place there," she said. "You should fill it up, and take it out when you need it."

27   As he grew up, Ralph took her advice. While other boys of seven or eight went to the movies, he sat in the Winsted courthouse, listening to the lawyers. While other children were reading comic books, he was reading the *Congressional Record*. These lengthy reports of everything that happened in the United States Congress bore most people. But to young Ralph, they were as interesting as the talk around the family supper table.

28   Ralph's parents sent him to good schools. He was graduated with high honors from Princeton University. Three years later, he earned a law degree from Harvard.

29   Most young lawyers from Harvard take jobs that pay a great deal of money. But Ralph Nader didn't care about money. He had more important things on his mind.

Writing Details

3. This part of the story tells you about Ralph Nader's family and his childhood. On a separate sheet, write the sentence that says:
   a. where his father and mother were born
   b. when Ralph was born
   c. what his father liked to talk about

4. You read two examples of Nathra's game "What if . . . ?" In your own words, write one of the examples given in the story.

Part III

30   **In 1966, Ralph Nader** began to speak up for ordinary citizens. He wrote about the danger of dirty or diseased meat sold by the big meat-packing companies. He gathered facts about the threat of explosions in natural gas pipelines. He suggested ways to protect the health and safety of coal miners. In these and other ways, he tried to protect the rights of consumers—the millions of men, women, and children who buy and use things.

31   In the late 1960s, the United States Congress passed a number of laws for which he had worked. The sad truth, however, is that most of these laws did little good. It is one thing to pass a law. It is another thing to make it work.

32   The government departments and agencies that were supposed to make these laws work were hardly doing their jobs. They had too little money and not enough people working for them. Also, the people running government agencies are often used to putting the needs of big companies before those of the ordinary citizen.

33   Big companies have the power and money to influence government. In fact, the heads of government departments and agencies are often former heads of big companies. As a result, laws that favor big companies are more likely to be passed, while laws that big companies don't like are sometimes not enforced.

34   Ralph Nader did not just complain that the government wasn't enforcing its own laws. He did something about it. In the summer of 1968, he hired seven young lawyers. "I want you to look into the government agency in charge of trade and business," he told them. "After you find out why this agency isn't doing its job properly, write a report." A newspaper writer called these young lawyers "Nader's Raiders," and the name stuck.

35   This time there were real results. The *Nader Report on the Federal Trade Commission* shook up that agency like a bomb. The head of the agency was replaced. Sweeping changes were made in the way the agency was run. From a sleepy, do-nothing government agency, it was changed

into an active one that really helped protect the American people.

36   After this first success, more Nader's Raiders went to work. They studied other government agencies. They even gathered facts about every member of the United States Congress. Out of each study came a report that was widely read.

37   Over the years, Ralph formed many other consumer education and action groups, such as Public Citizen, the Center for Study of Responsive Law, and Public Interest Research Groups, that now operate in 26 states and two provinces of Canada. They tackle problems in such areas as taxes, public health, and safety in the nation's nuclear-energy program. All these groups have one thing in common. They are part of Ralph's plan to broaden his work from a one-man operation to a national movement.

38   During the early 1980s, Ralph Nader was less active than usual as personal problems—illness and the death of his older brother—slowed him down. Before long, however, he was back in the news, as famous as ever. Speaking all over California in 1988, he helped win stricter regulation of car insurance rates in that state. He used his influence to help defeat a proposed 50% pay raise in Congress. For 19 years, he had fought to require safety air bags in cars. Finally, in 1989, he won his long battle. The three major automobile companies agreed to install the safety devices in their new cars.

39   Today he is still the guiding spirit behind a large network of public-interest groups that operate with a budget of five million dollars. All over the country, thousands of people help out in his various organizations. Over a hundred of his staff members work in Washington, D.C. But none of them works harder than Ralph Nader himself.

40   He generally works seven days a week, eighteen hours a day, and sleeps only four hours a night. He has

never married. He does not own a house, a car, or a television set. He has little time to be a private citizen because he is too busy working as a public citizen.

41   What does he believe in? What does he want? He wants to make government and business work better for more Americans. He has never forgotten what his father used to say: "Citizens must give more to their country than they take from it." To do this, Ralph Nader believes, every private citizen must become a public citizen.

Finding the Main Idea

5. The main idea of paragraph 40 is best expressed by sentence:
   (*a*) 1   (*b*) 2   (*c*) 3   (*d*) 4

6. Which of the following sentences about Ralph Nader best expresses the main idea of paragraph 30?
   a. He wrote about dangers caused by the big meat-packing companies.
   b. He won his fight against General Motors.
   c. He worked on a variety of problems that affect consumers.
   d. He cared about the health and safety of coal miners.

Working with Words

7. The word *private* (paragraph 10) means:
   (*a*) known to all   (*b*) known to only a few
   (*c*) highly respected   (*d*) low-ranking

8. Examples of *ordinary* (paragraph 30) citizens are most people's:
   (*a*) favorite TV stars   (*b*) friends and neighbors
   (*c*) state senators   (*d*) cartoon heroes

9. A law that is not *enforced* (paragraph 33) is likely to be:
   (*a*) feared   (*b*) remembered   (*c*) unwritten   (*d*) disobeyed

10. The word *famous* (paragraph 38) is most closely related to the word:
    (*a*) fame   (*b*) family   (*c*) famished   (*d*) famine

EXERCISES

Putting Events in Sequence

A.   Write the letters of each set of events in the order in which the events happened in Ralph Nader's life. For example, would you answer #1 by writing *a-b* or *b-a?* If you need help, look back at the story.

1. *a.* Ralph Nader gets a law degree from Harvard.
   b. He listens to lawyers argue cases in the courthouse of Winsted, Connecticut.

2. *a.* He writes *Unsafe at Any Speed.*
   b. General Motors hires detectives to find out about him.

3. *a.* The United States Senate passes the National Traffic and Motor Vehicle Safety Act.
   b. Two detectives are caught following Ralph Nader.

4. *a.* He hires seven young lawyers.
   b. Nader's Raiders report on the Federal Trade Commission.

5. *a.* Nathra and Rose Nader come to live in America.
   b. Ralph Nader sets up Public Interest Research Groups.

Making Inferences

B.   Use what you have read about Ralph Nader to infer, or figure out, the correct choice.

1. The publication of *Unsafe at Any Speed* displeased:
   (*a*) the public   (*b*) automobile makers   (*c*) Ralph Nader
   (*d*) the United States government

2. Which of the following is an inference?
   (*a*) Ralph Nader's parents were born in Lebanon.
   (*b*) The Nader family lived in Winsted, Connecticut.
   (*c*) Ralph's life work made his parents proud of him.
   (*d*) Ralph attended both Princeton and Harvard.

3. Nathra Nader's game "What if . . . ?" was designed to:
   (*a*) show how clever he was
   (*b*) prove that big business is bad
   (*c*) teach others to think for themselves
   (*d*) make fun of the government

4. Which of the following opinions would Ralph Nader hold?
   (*a*) More government regulation of business is needed.
   (*b*) Less regulation is needed.
   (*c*) No regulation is needed.
   (*d*) No amount of regulation will help the consumer.

Understanding Cause and Effect

   C.   Write the letter of the best choice.

1. Ralph Nader first became widely known because of:
   (*a*) the report on the Federal Trade Commission
   (*b*) Harvard University
   (*c*) Winsted, Connecticut
   (*d*) General Motors

2. Which was a cause of his lifelong concern with public issues?
   (*a*) his parents
   (*b*) his law degree from Harvard
   (*c*) Nader's Raiders
   (*d*) Public Citizen

3. General Motors tried to harm Ralph Nader's reputation because of:
   (*a*) the publication of *Unsafe at Any Speed*
   (*b*) the attack in that book on the Corvair
   (*c*) Ralph's work for a law on safety standards for automobiles
   (*d*) all of the above

4. Changes in the Federal Trade Commission resulted from:
   (*a*) the work of the Center for Study of Responsive Law
   (*b*) a report by Nader's Raiders
   (*c*) the publication of *Unsafe at Any Speed*
   (*d*) a speech by Ralph Nader

Separating Fact from Opinion

    D.   Tell which is a *fact* and which is an *opinion*.

1. Ralph wanted safety air bags installed in cars.

2. He would make a good President of the United States.

3. He is a threat to the American way of life.

4. He has been concerned about safety in automobiles.

Choosing the Best Title

    E.   Write the number of the best title for the story of Ralph Nader.

1. The Richest Man in America

2. The Man Who Made Government and Business Work Better

3. A Lawyer From Connecticut

4. Unsafe at Any Speed.

Speaking, Listening, and Writing

    F.   Be prepared to discuss one of the following topics with your classmates.

1. What kinds of things do you think should be improved where you live?

2. Tell about somebody you know or know about who has tried to improve things where you live. (You may wish to make up a name for the real person you choose to tell about.)

    G.   Write a paragraph or more about one of the following topics.

1. How did Ralph Nader's parents influence him?

2. What part did General Motors play in his life?

3. What are some of the problems on which he has worked?

America's greatest woman airplane pilot faces death in the sky.

3. Amelia Earhart

Part I

1   **People used to say,** "It's a man's world." After the first successful airplane flight, even the sky seemed to belong to men. All the famous pilots were men. All but one!

2   For a few years, a young American woman showed that flying is not just for men. She also did more than anyone else to interest women in aviation, or flying. Her name, famous everywhere, was Amelia Earhart.

3   She was born in Kansas in 1898, five years before the first airplane flight. Like other girls of her time, Amelia learned to cook and sew. But she also learned to use tools, to play baseball, and to explore the wonders of nature. Amelia grew up eager to live her own life and make something of it.

4   In 1920, she moved with her parents to California. There something special came into Amelia's life—the thrill of flying. By this time, more people were learning to fly. Air shows, stunt flying, and airplane races were becoming popular, and Amelia went to see as many of them as she could. To her, flying seemed wonderful.

5   At the supper table one evening, she told her parents, "I've decided to learn how to fly an airplane."

6   "But, Amelia, I've never heard of a woman pilot," her mother protested.

7   "I can learn to fly as well as any man," her daughter said. "I know I can."

8   Mr. Earhart smiled at his daughter's words. "I understand the cost of flying lessons can add up to a thousand dollars," he said. "Where will all that money come from?"

9   "I'll manage somehow," Amelia replied. "I've already taken a job."

10   Making enough money for flying lessons, however, was not easy. To earn money, she worked as a clerk for the telephone company and then as a photographer, a miner, and a truck driver. It took a long time to earn enough for a flying lesson. When she didn't have the money, her teacher sometimes gave her a lesson anyway.

11   In May 1923, she finally got her pilot's license. With her mother's help, she had bought a second-hand airplane. Whenever she could, she flew her airplane and learned more about aviation.

12   Three years later, she took a job as a social worker in Boston, Massachusetts. Like her earlier jobs, it was chiefly a way to earn money for flying. In her free time, she continued to read about aviation and talk with other pilots about flying. She spent almost every weekend in the place she loved best—up in the sky.

13   People respected and admired Amelia for her knowledge of aviation and her enthusiasm for flying. She made friends and was elected vice-president of the Boston branch of a national aviation club. She was winning a name for herself as one of the best pilots around, male or female.

Finding Details

1. Give the number of the paragraph in which you learn:
   a. when and where Amelia Earhart was born
   b. different things she did as a young girl in Kansas

c. how much flying lessons cost

d. when she received her pilot's license

2. This part of the story mentions three states in which Amelia lived. Give the numbers of the paragraphs that provide these details.

Part II

14   **One day, Amelia received** a mysterious telephone call that changed her life.

15   "Hello, Miss Earhart?" a man's voice asked. "My name is Captain Hilton H. Railey. Would you be interested in doing something dangerous but very important for aviation?"

16   As a result of that telephone call, Amelia became the first woman to cross the Atlantic Ocean in an airplane. On that flight in June 1928, she was only a passenger. Another pilot, Wilbur Stultz, was at the controls for the trip.

17   Even though a man had done the flying, this was an important event for women. Overnight, Amelia became famous. Newspaper reporters wrote down whatever she said. Crowds followed her wherever she went. There were parades, speeches, and medals in her honor.

18   Why did the world heap such fame and glory upon Amelia Earhart? There were at least two reasons.

19   A year earlier, in 1927, Charles Lindbergh had made the first daring solo flight across the Atlantic Ocean. Taking off from New York City, he had landed in Paris, France. The public went wild over this handsome young American pilot. "Lindy" became the greatest hero of his time. Now the public was ready for another hero. But a heroine, a woman as brave as "Lindy," would be even better.

20   Amelia was tall and slim, almost boyish looking. Her blond hair was cut short in an easy, natural style. She was outgoing and friendly, yet this young woman was also modest and soft-spoken. Some people felt that

Amelia even looked like Charles Lindbergh. Newspapers called her "Lady Lindy."

21   Amelia wrote two popular books about her life and her flight across the Atlantic. She became the aviation editor of *Cosmopolitan* magazine. Over a million American women read her articles about flying. She also urged women to try other careers.

22   In 1931, she married a book publisher, George Putnam. He understood his wife's desire to fly. As a result, they each enjoyed their chosen careers in publishing and aviation. They had a happy marriage.

23   It seemed as if Amelia's fame and good fortune would never end. As one reporter described her, she was "a girl who has everything—youth, intelligence, beauty, personality, and a promising future." What more could anyone want?

24   Yet all these honors made her strangely uneasy. After all, she had been only a passenger on that flight across the Atlantic. "I was just baggage," she said, "like a sack of potatoes." To deserve her fame, she felt that she must make the same flight alone.

25   Amelia had another important reason to fly solo over the Atlantic, as Lindbergh had done. She wanted to prove that whatever men could do, women could do, too.

Writing Details

3. Write the missing name in each of the following sentences. If you need help, look back at Part II of the story.
   a. The first person to fly solo across the Atlantic Ocean was
      _____.
   b. _____ asked Amelia to cross the Atlantic by airplane.
   c. _____ was the pilot of the plane that carried Amelia.
   d. The book publisher who married Amelia was _____.

4. A reporter wrote that Amelia was "a girl who has everything." List the five things that this reporter mentioned.

Part III

26   **On the evening of** May 20, 1932, Amelia took off alone in a red Lockheed airplane from the coast of Canada. She was headed for England. Before her stretched miles and miles of lonely ocean.

27   All through this night flight, danger and death rode with her. First, her altimeter broke. (An altimeter shows a pilot how high the airplane is flying.) This was serious trouble. In the dark, she had no way of knowing how close she was to the ocean.

28   Next she flew into a violent storm. Strong winds shook the little airplane and tossed it about in the air. All around her, bolts of lightning crashed.

29   When she finally flew out of the storm, Amelia faced a new danger. Suddenly, flames shot out from a broken part of her engine. Her heart almost stopped beating. What if the flames burned through the metal to the rest of the engine? Or what if the gasoline caught on fire?

30   There was nothing she could do but go on. All through the night, she flew, tensely watching the deadly flames.

31   With the dawn came more trouble. One of the tanks on her airplane was leaking gasoline. Clearly, she couldn't reach England. So Amelia headed for the closest land—Ireland.

32   Would she make it even to Ireland? Minutes passed as she stared into the gray distance. Her hope, like her luck, was fast giving out. Then she sighted land.

33   Circling about, she looked for a place to bring down her airplane. At last, she landed safely, bumping and bouncing, in a farmer's field.

34   The dangerous flight was over. Amelia had flown 2,026 miles in only 14 hours and 56 minutes. It was a new world record for crossing the Atlantic.

35   Newspaper headlines read: "AMELIA FLIES THE ATLANTIC!"

36   The people and governments of Europe acclaimed Amelia. A new flood of honors and awards swept over her. Kings, presidents, and other heads of state showered more medals and praise upon her. With her husband, she made a grand tour of England and several countries in Europe.

37   Back in America, she was invited to dinner one evening at the White House. President Franklin Delano Roosevelt and his wife Eleanor were delighted with her visit. During the evening, the talk naturally turned to flying. Amelia told Mrs. Roosevelt how wonderful flying was—especially at night.

38   "I have never flown in an airplane at night," Eleanor Roosevelt said.

39   "Would you like to—tonight?" asked Amelia.

40   The First Lady did not think twice about it. "Why, I'd love to!"

41   A little later that same evening, the two women were up in the sky together. Amelia, still wearing her fancy white party gloves, was at the controls of the airplane.

42   The next day, the story was in all the newspapers. Eleanor Roosevelt was the First Lady of the Land, but Amelia Earhart was truly the First Lady of the Air.

Finding the Main Idea

5. The main idea of paragraph 36 is best expressed by sentence:
(*a*) 1   (*b*) 2   (*c*) 3   (*d*) 4

6. Which of the following sentences best expresses the main idea of paragraphs 27–30?
(*a*) All through this night flight, danger and death rode with her.
(*b*) All through the night, she flew, tensely watching the deadly flames.
(*c*) When she finally flew out of the storm, Amelia faced a new danger.
(*d*) There was nothing she could do but go on.

Part IV

43   **"What will you do next?"** reporters asked Amelia.

44   An even greater flight filled her dreams. This time she would fly all the way around the world.

45   On June 1, 1937, she set off on the longest flight of all. With her was Fred Noonan, her navigator, whose job was to lead the airplane in the right direction.

46   Starting from Miami, Florida, she flew east from country to country. On June 30, she reached the large island of New Guinea in the Pacific Ocean. Her next

stop for fuel and rest was to be tiny Howland Island, no more than a dot on the map, 2,550 miles across the ocean from New Guinea.

47 The United States Coast Guard ship *Itasca* waited next to Howland Island. Its purpose was to guide Amelia's airplane by radio across the ocean to the island.

48 July 2, 1937. Dawn came, but no sign of the airplane. The wide blue sky was empty.

49 At 7:42 in the morning, Amelia's voice came over the radio. "We must be on you, but cannot see you. Gas is running low. Have been unable to reach you by radio. We are flying at altitude one thousand feet."

50 Something was wrong with the radio in her airplane. If she couldn't receive messages from the *Itasca*, she might never find the tiny island.

51 A little later, the men on the ship heard her voice again. "We are circling but cannot see you."

52 At 8:45 her last message came through. Her voice sounded choked with worry. "We are in a line of position 157 degrees—337 degrees. We are running north and south."

53 That was the last anyone ever heard from Amelia. Almost at once, the entire world knew that she had been lost at sea.

54 The United States Navy began an all-out search for the missing airplane. Joining the *Itasca* were an aircraft carrier, a battleship, several destroyers, and other ships and airplanes. They covered thousands of miles of ocean. They searched every island where the two fliers might have landed. But the airplane was never found.

55 Despite some recent findings, the mystery of Amelia Earhart's fate may never be solved. But we do know how she felt about her last flight. In a letter to her husband, she wrote: "Please know that I am quite aware of the hazards. I want to do it because I want to do it. Women must try to do things as men have tried. When they fail, their failure must be a challenge to others."

Working with Words

7. A *navigator* (paragraph 45) would most likely use a:
   (*a*) newspaper   (*b*) gun   (*c*) map   (*d*) screwdriver

8. The word *altitude* (paragraph 49) has to do with:
   (*a*) size   (*b*) height   (*c*) speed   (*d*) direction

9. Which of the following words is closest in meaning to *hazards* (paragraph 55)?
   (*a*) dangers   (*b*) choices   (*c*) storms   (*d*) delights

10. By a *"challenge* (paragraph 55) to others," Amelia Earhart meant a:
    (*a*) dispute   (*b*) dare   (*c*) command   (*d*) disappointment

EXERCISES

Putting Events in Sequence

A. Write the letters of each set of events in the order in which the events happened in Amelia Earhart's life. For example, would you answer #1 by writing *a-b* or *b-a*? If you need help, look back at the story.

1. *a.* Amelia is born in Kansas.
   b. The airplane is invented.

2. *a.* She flies from America to England for the first time.
   b. She writes two popular books on flying.

3. *a.* She makes a solo flight across the Atlantic Ocean.
   b. Charles Lindbergh makes a solo flight across the Atlantic Ocean.

4. *a.* She takes Mrs. Roosevelt on an airplane flight at night.
   b. Amelia and her husband make a grand tour of England and Europe.

5. *a.* Amelia Earhart and Fred Noonan set off on a flight together.
   b. Amelia decides to fly around the world.

Making Inferences

B.   Use what you have read about Amelia Earhart to infer, or figure out, the correct choice.

1. Amelia's great popularity was probably helped by her:
   - (a) parents
   - (b) husband
   - (c) political opinions
   - (d) physical appearance

2. From paragraphs 37–42, you can infer that Eleanor Roosevelt was:
   - (a) proud
   - (b) timid
   - (c) adventuresome
   - (d) misunderstood

3. The most reasonable inference about Amelia's last flight is that her airplane:
   - (a) landed on a Pacific island
   - (b) returned to New Guinea
   - (c) was hidden by the U.S. Navy
   - (d) crashed at sea

4. From her letter to her husband (paragraph 55), you can infer that Amelia:
   - (a) knew that she would survive all dangers
   - (b) loved her husband deeply
   - (c) wanted to encourage women to lead more challenging lives
   - (d) expected to fail

Understanding Cause and Effect

C.   Write the letter of the best choice.

1. Amelia made her solo flight across the Atlantic Ocean because:
   - (a) she needed more money
   - (b) her husband urged her to do it
   - (c) she wanted more fame
   - (d) she felt she should earn her fame

2. One cause of Amelia's popularity after her first flight across the Atlantic was:
   (*a*) the public's need for hero worship
   (*b*) her courage as a pilot
   (*c*) Lindbergh's praise of her
   (*d*) her knowledge of aviation

3. On her last flight, Amelia could not find the coast guard vessel *Itasca* because:
   (*a*) the fog was too dense
   (*b*) it was raining too hard
   (*c*) she was lost
   (*d*) she was flying too high

4. Amelia's disappearance on her flight around the world was caused by:
   (*a*) engine failure
   (*b*) a faulty radio
   (*c*) a tropical storm
   (*d*) a fire in her airplane

Separating Fact from Opinion

   D.   Tell which is a *fact* and which is an *opinion*.

1. A reporter once described Amelia as "a girl who has everything."

2. She was a beautiful young woman.

3. Fred Noonan was her navigator.

4. Women must try to do things as men have tried.

Choosing the Best Title

   E.   Write the number of the best title for the story of Amelia Earhart.

1. Alone Across the Atlantic

2. First Lady of the Air

3. The Lady Vanishes

4. Women in Aviation

Speaking, Listening, and Writing

F.   Be prepared to discuss one of the following topics with your classmates.

1. What do you think was the bravest thing Amelia did? Explain your answer.

2. What do you think Amelia would say to men and women who believe that a woman's place is only in the home? Would you agree or disagree with her?

G.   Write a paragraph or more about one of the following topics.

1. Write a letter to Amelia telling her why you think she was the perfect heroine for her time.

2. Pretend you are a newspaper reporter. In your own words, write a short news story on Amelia's solo flight across the Atlantic Ocean. Make up a headline for your news story.

3. Give evidence that Amelia was a brave woman.

One of baseball's finest players lends a helping hand to others.

4. Roberto Clemente

Part I

1   **One of the greatest** baseball players of all time was Roberto Clemente. For 18 years, he was the star outfielder and most powerful batter of the Pittsburgh Pirates.

2   Roberto was born in 1934 in a small town in Puerto Rico. Of the seven children in the Clemente family, he was the youngest. None of them loved baseball as much as he did. As a boy, he had only one thing on his mind—baseball!

3   Hour after hour, he would throw a rubber ball against the wall of his house and then catch it. He would squeeze a hard rubber ball in his right hand to make his throwing arm strong. When he walked down the dusty streets of his hometown, he would hit a tin can with a broomstick. Roberto lived baseball.

4   Sometimes he was so busy playing baseball with his friends that he forgot to come home to eat. One day, this made his mother angry.

5   "*Basta!*" ("Enough!") she cried.

6   She grabbed his baseball bat. To Roberto's horror, she threw it into the oven to burn it up. He snatched it out just in time.

7   In later years, however, Roberto remembered his

childhood as a happy one. He always spoke about his parents with pride and affection.

8   In high school, Roberto joined the track team. He learned to run fast and jump high. He also learned to throw the javelin, a long, pointed spear that flies through the air and sticks into the ground. Throwing the javelin helped make his right arm even stronger.

9   Although Roberto was shy in high school, he made one very good friend—his history teacher, Mrs. María Isabel Cáceres. He liked to visit her. At her home, he would listen to records of *danzas*, a popular form of music in Puerto Rico.

10   Mrs. Cáceres' husband was the coach of the high-school softball team. Roberto played outfield on this team. The coach could see that the young man was an unusually good baseball player. With the coach's help, Roberto joined a professional baseball team called the Santurce Crabbers.

11   The Santurce Crabbers was an important baseball team in Puerto Rico. During the winter, famous baseball stars such as Orlando Cepeda and Willie Mays played with the team. For three winters, Roberto played ball with the Santurce team. He served especially well as an outfielder, but he also became a strong batter with a high batting average.

12   A really good batter, one who can hit the ball three out of every 10 times at bat, is said to have a batting average of .300. During one winter with the Santurce team, Roberto batted .356!

Finding Details

1. Give the number of the paragraph that tells:
   a. when and where Roberto was born
   b. that he made a good friend in high school

c. which famous baseball players spent winters with the Santurce Crabbers

d. what Roberto's batting average was during one winter with
   the Santurce team

2. The number of the paragraph in which you learn who helped
   Roberto to join a professional baseball team is:
   (*a*) 1   (*b*) 4   (*c*) 10   (*d*) 11

Part II

13   **People began to take notice** of Roberto. Scouts from
nine baseball teams had their eyes on the young ballplayer.

14   In 1954, a scout for the Brooklyn Dodgers offered
him $10,000 to join that famous team. What a great
chance for a 19-year-old who had just finished high
school! Roberto said "yes" to the Brooklyn Dodgers
scout.

15   Later that day, a scout for the Milwaukee Braves
made an even better offer. His team would give the
young man $30,000 if he would join them.

16   Roberto didn't know what to do. He went home to
tell his mother and father what had happened. For his
mother, there was only one right thing to do. He had
already given his word to play with the Dodgers.

17   "If you gave your word," his mother said, "you keep
your word."

18   New baseball players are trained in the minor
leagues. If they are good enough, they move up to the
major leagues. So Roberto went to Montreal, Canada, to
play in a minor-league club of the Brooklyn Dodgers.

19   He was not happy there. In Montreal, most of the
people speak French. The men on the baseball team
spoke English. But Roberto, who spoke Spanish, knew
very little English and no French at all.

20   For the first time, he was living far from home in a strange country. Also, many black people live in Puerto Rico, but very few live in Canada. So for the first time, he learned what it was like to be a black man in a land of white people. He felt very lonely.

21   All this was hard enough for the young man. But something else happened that really upset him.

22   For many years, only white players had been allowed to play major-league baseball. Then in 1947, the great black player Jackie Robinson had broken the racial barrier in baseball. Seven years later, however, there was still a kind of unofficial quota in the major leagues. Only a small number of black baseball players were allowed to play in each major-league team.

23   The Brooklyn Dodgers already had some black players in their major-league club. This is why they kept Roberto in their minor-league club. At that time, though, a major-league baseball team could draft, or take, a good player from another team's minor-league club. Thus, the Brooklyn Dodgers were in danger of losing Roberto to some other ball team if they didn't move him up to the major league.

24   What could the Brooklyn Dodgers do? Without telling him why, they tried to "hide" their valuable new player.

25   Whenever he played well, the manager of the team took him out of the ball game. Whenever he played badly, the manager left him in the game. Roberto couldn't understand what was happening to him.

26   The plan didn't work after all. A scout for the Pittsburgh Pirates spotted the young man. The scout knew a great baseball player when he saw one.

27   In November 1954, the Pirates drafted Roberto Clemente for their major-league team. For the next 18 years, he played right field with that team.

Writing Details

3. Can you pick out the facts in paragraph 14 of this part? Write:
   a. how old Roberto was when he finished high school
   b. the year in which a Brooklyn Dodgers scout made him an offer
   c. how much money the Dodgers scout offered
   d. what Roberto's reply was

4. Write *T* if a statement is true or *F* if it is false.
   a. Most people in Montreal speak French.
   b. The men on Roberto's team spoke French.
   c. Roberto did not speak French at all.
   d. Roberto did not speak English at all.

Part III

28   **Although Roberto was now** a major-league baseball player, his troubles were not over. In fact, they were just beginning.

29   One of his brothers was sick and dying in Puerto Rico. Before Roberto began his first season with the Pirates, he visited his brother in the hospital. As Roberto drove away from the hospital, a drunken driver hit his car at high speed. The young ballplayer's back was hurt in the crash. This was only the first of many times in his life that he was hurt or sick.

30   In later years, he suffered from pulled muscles, chipped bones, and two serious illnesses. He also had many headaches and stomachaches and much trouble sleeping at night. Baseball sports writers called him "Mr. Aches and Pains."

31   It seemed that the worse Roberto felt, the better he played baseball. By the end of his first five years with the Pirates, he had become a powerful player.

32   As a right fielder, he kept many batters from scoring. He ran as fast as a racer and leaped high to catch fly balls. Often he would slam into the fence or climb right up the back wall of the ballfield to turn a home run into an out. He could fire the ball back to home plate from 420 feet away. He had the strongest throwing arm of any outfielder in baseball.

33   As a batter, Roberto gave pitchers bad dreams. Most batters wait for a good pitch. But not Roberto! He would hit any kind of pitch.

34   Somebody once asked a pitcher for the Brooklyn Dodgers if there was any way to keep Roberto Clemente from hitting.

35   "Sure," the pitcher answered with a grin. "Roll the ball on the ground."

Finding the Main Idea

5. The main idea of paragraph 32 concerns Roberto's:
  (*a*) strong throwing arm
  (*b*) speed in the outfield
  (*c*) skills as a right fielder
  (*d*) abilities as a batter

6. Which of the following sentences about Roberto Clemente best expresses the main idea of Part III?
  (*a*) He had many accidents and illnesses.
  (*b*) He became a powerful baseball player.
  (*c*) Before he had many accidents and illnesses, he was a powerful baseball player.
  (*d*) Although he had many accidents and illnesses, he became a powerful baseball player.

Part IV

36   **Roberto was not only** a great baseball player. He was also a man who cared very much about other people and tried to help them. Over the years, he always sent part of the money he earned home to his parents.

37   "My folks took care of me when I was young," he said. "Now they are old, and I can take care of them."

38   Roberto loved children. He often visited sick boys and girls in hospitals all over Puerto Rico. He hoped that his own success in baseball would help Puerto Rican children.

39   For many years, he dreamed of helping young people by building a Sports City in Puerto Rico. His plan was to get the best coaches to teach many different sports. In that way, every boy and girl would be able to find at least one sport to learn and play.

40   "They spend millions of dollars for dope control in

Puerto Rico," he said, "but they attack the problem after the problem is there. Why don't they attack it before it starts? You try to get kids so they don't become dope addicts, and it would help to get them interested in sports and give them somewhere to learn to play them."

41   In December 1972, a powerful earthquake struck the city of Managua, Nicaragua, in Central America. During an earthquake, the ground shakes and sometimes splits open in cracks. Buildings fall, and there are fires. This earthquake killed over 10,000 people. Almost a quarter of a million people lost their homes.

42   Roberto wanted to help. Knowing that food, clothing, and medicine would be needed, he set to work. On radio and television, he asked the people of Puerto Rico to give whatever they could. Nobody was more loved and admired on the island than Roberto. In a few days, the people gave $150,000 and about 26 tons of supplies.

43   The supplies were loaded onto an airplane, which made two flights to Nicaragua. On New Year's Eve, Roberto decided to go along on the third flight. He wanted to be sure that the food and clothing reached the people who needed them.

44   A little after 9 o'clock at night, the airplane took off from the airport at San Juan, Puerto Rico, and headed out over the water. Suddenly, the airplane crashed nose-first into the sea. In a few minutes, it sank out of sight.

45   Nobody knew what had gone wrong. Although ships and divers searched the area for many days, they never found any trace of Roberto.

46   Baseball had lost one of its finest players. Three months after he died, Roberto was given an extraordinary honor. He was chosen to belong to baseball's Hall of Fame.

47   The people of Puerto Rico had lost one of their most beloved heroes. As they still say, *"Era un gran hombre— un hombre de buen corazón."* ("He was a great man—a man of good heart.") Truly, that was Roberto Clemente.

Working with Words

7. A *barrier* (paragraph 22) is most like a door that is:
   (*a*) open　(*b*) missing　(*c*) broken　(*d*) closed

8. With a *quota* (paragraph 22), persons or things are:
   (*a*) unlimited　(*b*) limited　(*c*) forbidden　(*d*) required

9. *Addicts* (paragraph 40) are most like:
   (*a*) kings　(*b*) bosses　(*c*) slaves　(*d*) heros

10. The meaning of *extraordinary* (paragraph 46) is best expressed by:
    (*a*) unusual　(*b*) usual　(*c*) unnecessary　(*d*) necessary

---

EXERCISES

Putting Events in Sequence

A.　Write the letters of each set of events in the order in which the events happened in Roberto Clemente's life. For example, would you answer #1 by writing *a-b* or *b-a*? If you need help, look back at the story.

1. *a.* Roberto's mother tries to burn his baseball bat.
   b. Roberto joins the Santurce Crabbers.

2. *a.* He signs up to play with the Brooklyn Dodgers.
   b. He becomes friends with Mrs. María Cáceres.

3. *a.* The Pittsburgh Pirates draft him.
   b. The Brooklyn Dodgers keep him "hidden" in their minor-league club in Canada.

4. *a.* His back is badly hurt in a car crash in Puerto Rico.
   b. He tries to help the people of Managua, Nicaragua.

5. *a.* He is chosen to join baseball's Hall of Fame.
   b. He is lost at sea in an airplane crash.

Making Inferences

B. Use what you have learned about Roberto Clemente to infer, or figure out, the correct choice.

1. During most of his career, Roberto played baseball with the:
   (a) Santurce Crabbers   (b) Brooklyn Dodgers
   (c) Pittsburgh Pirates   (d) Montreal Expos

2. Roberto looked upon his parents' opinions with:
   (a) scorn   (b) anger   (c) indifference   (d) respect

3. Which solution to the problem of drugs would Roberto be most likely to favor?
   (a) Offer drug addicts treatment.
   (b) Start early to prevent drug addiction.
   (c) Put drug pushers in jail.
   (d) Legalize drugs.

4. With which of the following statements would Roberto probably agree?
   (a) Making lots of money is what matters.
   (b) Helping other people makes life worth living.
   (c) Look out for yourself first.
   (d) Don't expect help from others.

Understanding Cause and Effect

C. Write the letter of the best choice.

1. Roberto joined the Brooklyn Dodgers because:
   (a) they offered the most money
   (b) he promised that he would
   (c) no other team asked him
   (d) he wanted to leave Puerto Rico

2. Roberto's power as a baseball player was a result of:
   (a) the help of his parents
   (b) good luck
   (c) years of practice
   (d) a lifetime of good health

3. The cause of the crash that killed Roberto was:
   (*a*) pilot error   (*b*) an overloaded airplane
   (*c*) bad weather   (*d*) unknown

4. The effect, or result, of the Brooklyn Dodgers' scheme to "hide" Roberto was:
   (*a*) he went back to Puerto Rico
   (*b*) they lost him anyway
   (*c*) he remained in their minor-league club for years
   (*d*) he moved up to their major-league club anyway

Separating Fact from Opinion

D.   Tell which is a *fact* and which is an *opinion*.

1. Of all sports, baseball is best.

2. Of all sports, Roberto liked baseball best.

3. Roberto played right field with the Pittsburgh Pirates.

4. Right field is certainly the most difficult position to play in baseball.

Choosing the Best Title

E.   Write the number of the best title for the story of Roberto Clemente.

1. Sports in Puerto Rico

2. The Nicaraguan Earthquake

3. The Great-Hearted Baseball Player

4. Quotas in Baseball

Speaking, Listening, and Writing

F. Listen while several of your classmates discuss one of the following topics. Be prepared to tell whose ideas you agree with most—and why. (*Hint:* It may help if you take notes while you listen.)

1. What was Roberto's idea about how to end drug addiction among young people? Do you think this idea could work?

2. Suppose you became a rich and respected superstar. How would you use your money and fame to try to help other people?

G. Write a paragraph or more about one of the following topics.

1. What made Roberto such an unusual baseball player?

2. Tell how Roberto helped other people.

3. Tell about Roberto's troubles during the years he played minor-league baseball in Canada.

A pioneer in women's rights believes "failure is impossible."

5. Susan B. Anthony

Part I

1 **It was a bright summer morning** in the little town of Canandaigua, New York. In the courthouse, a large crowd waited. The people had come for the trial of the famous Susan B. Anthony.

2 "I expected to see a tough woman smoking a big black cigar—like the cartoons of her in the newspapers," said a man in the crowd. "But she looks nice in that dark dress and white collar."

3 "Sh!" a woman whispered. "The trial is about to start."

4 And so began, on June 17, 1873, the case of the United States government against Susan B. Anthony.

5 Why was this woman on trial? What had she done? She was on trial because, in a national election the year before, she had dared to vote!

6 In those days, a woman was not allowed to vote. But that was not all. When a woman married, any property she owned became her husband's, not hers. If she earned money, her husband collected it. A married woman could not sign contracts. If her husband divorced her, she could not even have charge of her own children. At that time, a woman had hardly any of the legal rights she has today.

7   A woman was not considered a man's equal in any way. Her place was only in the home. She was not supposed to go about in public without a man. Most women could not expect to go to college.

8   "What use is a higher education," people said in those days, "to someone whose only purpose in life is to be a mother and a housewife?"

9   For most of her life, Susan B. Anthony fought for equal rights for women. In those early years, she was the driving force behind the women's rights movement.

Finding Details

1. Write the number of the paragraph in which you learn:
   a. when the trial of Susan B. Anthony took place
   b. where the trial took place
   c. why the trial took place
   d. how Susan looked at the trial

2. You learn about things that a woman was *not* allowed to do a hundred years ago in paragraphs:
   (*a*) 1 and 2   (*b*) 4 and 5   (*c*) 6 and 7   (*d*) 8 and 9

Part II

10   **The first battle for women's rights** was fought in New York State. Susan planned to ask the state lawmakers—the legislature—to give women the vote. She would also ask them to give married women the right to own property, to sign contracts, and to have charge of their children after a divorce.

11   Such ideas were unheard of. Susan had to show the lawmakers that many people in New York State wanted

women to have these rights. All through the winter of 1853–1854, she traveled from town to town across the state, making speeches. She urged people to sign a petition, a formal paper asking the lawmakers to pass a law for women's rights. Other women helped her gather names for the petition.

12   In those days, women—especially unmarried women like Susan—were not supposed to travel alone. And for a woman to make speeches in public, as she did, was simply shocking!

13   At these public meetings, most men made fun of her or shouted at her to go home and do her housework. Men often threatened her. Some even threw rotten fruit and vegetables at her.

14   Many women looked down their noses at her. "*Nice* women," they said, "don't need an equal rights law. *They* have husbands to take care of them!"

15   Despite this opposition, she kept on making speeches and asking people to sign her petition. In the end, Susan and her helpers collected 10,000 names on the petition. How could they fail?

16   Yet the lawmakers—all men, of course—laughed at the very idea of giving women equal rights with men. The New York State Legislature beat down the equal rights law. It never had a chance. But Susan was not beaten down.

17   "We will be back," she told the lawmakers. "We will be back again and again until the laws are passed giving women their due rights."

18   And she did come back. All through the coldest New York winter in years, she again plodded from town to town. She spoke in churches and schoolhouses, and she collected even more names for her petition.

19   Again Susan returned to the legislature. And again it voted down the proposed law. It took her seven years of hard work and heartbreak, but at last, in 1860, the law was passed in New York State. Though women still

could not vote, they had won the other important rights. Now married women could own their own property, sign contracts, and have charge of their children after a divorce. No one worked harder for these rights than Susan B. Anthony.

20   In 1861, the Civil War began. With the nation torn apart over the problem of slavery, women's rights had to take second place. All during the war, Susan worked as hard against slavery as she had worked for women's rights.

21   When the war was over, the right of black Americans to vote was protected for the first time by two amendments—changes in the United States Constitution. The 14th and 15th Amendments did not say anything about the right of women to vote. However, the 15th Amendment began with these words: "The right of citizens of the United States to vote shall not be denied. . . ." And that gave Susan a daring idea.

Writing Details

3. List three rights that Susan asked the New York State lawmakers to give women.

4. What right was *not* given to women by:
    a. the New York State equal rights law of 1860
    b. the 14th and 15th Amendments to the U.S. Constitution

Part III

22   **Susan was visiting** one of her sisters in Rochester, New York, late in October of 1872. A notice in a newspaper caught her eye. It reminded citizens to register

right away so that they could vote in the next week's national election.

23   She knew that the notice was meant only for men. But the 15th Amendment spoke of "the right of citizens of the United States." Weren't women also citizens?

24   On November 1, she led 15 well-dressed, respectable Rochester women into the voter registration office. Among the women were her three sisters—Hannah, Mary, and Guelma.

25   "Good day, ladies," said one of the men in the office. "What can we do for you?"

26   "We are here to register," Susan replied.

27   "R-r-register!" the man stuttered. "That's impossible. It's against the law."

28   She reached into her large handbag. From it, she pulled out a copy of the United States Constitution. Slowly and calmly, she read both the 14th and 15th Amendments to the surprised men.

29   "Now," she said, "show me where it says that women may not vote."

30   The men looked at the two amendments. Then they looked at one another. Not knowing what else to do, they allowed all the women to sign their names in the big book. In the next day or two, about 35 more women registered in other parts of Rochester.

31   The women returned to vote on November 5, Election Day. Once again, the men tried to stop them. But there were the names of all the women, neatly signed in the big registration book. While the men looked on, angry but helpless, each of the women voted.

32   You would think that a foreign army had invaded America! Newspaper headlines screamed the story across the nation. In the churches, the ministers preached sermons against Susan B. Anthony. The United States government knew that it had to act firmly. If nothing were done, a woman, by one bold act, would have won the vote for women all over America.

33   On November 28, the women who had voted were arrested, but they were not put into jail. Instead, the government decided to put only Miss Anthony on trial. Everyone knew that she was the real troublemaker.

34   After many delays, the famous trial began on June 17, 1873. The government put Judge Ward Hunt on the case. Because he wanted Susan to be found guilty, he would not let her speak in her own defense. He constantly ruled her lawyer "out of order." But the worst was yet to come.

35   At the end of the trial, Judge Hunt turned to the jury. He told them that by voting, Susan had broken the law. Now she must be punished.

36   "I therefore direct," the judge said slowly, "that you find a verdict of guilty."

37   Before anything could be said or done, Judge Hunt dismissed the jury. The trial was over. Susan had not been found guilty by a jury. She had been found guilty only by the men in government who were afraid that she would win the vote for women. The next day, Judge

Hunt ordered her to pay a fine of $100 and the cost of the trial.

38   "May it please your honor," she told him, "I shall never pay a dollar of your unjust penalty." And she never did.

Finding the Main Idea

5. The main idea of paragraph 31 is best expressed by sentence:
   (*a*) 1   (*b*) 2   (*c*) 3   (*d*) 4

6. Paragraphs 34–38 tell about the trial of Susan B. Anthony. Which of the following sentences best expresses the main idea of these five paragraphs?
   (*a*) Susan should have been allowed to speak in her own defense.
   (*b*) The government assigned Judge Ward Hunt to her case.
   (*c*) Judge Hunt ordered her to pay a fine of $100 and the cost of the trial.
   (*d*) She was found guilty in an unfair trial.

Part IV

39   **Although Susan had lost** the case, her trial helped the cause of women's suffrage, or right to vote. People all over the country wrote letters of sympathy to her and also sent her money.

40   All this support encouraged her. She decided to work for an amendment to the United States Constitution that would give women the vote.

41   For many years, she spoke in state after state for women's suffrage. When she was 72 years old, she became president of the National American Woman Suf-

frage Association. Wherever she went, the slim, gray-haired old woman, a red shawl around her shoulders, became a familiar and honored figure.

42   Susan made speeches for women's suffrage to labor unions in America. At a meeting in Germany, she spoke to women from many nations. She visited England to speak and work for the cause of votes for women.

43   Back in America, Susan went to a large meeting in honor of her 86th birthday. To a cheering crowd, she spoke her last public words: "Failure is impossible."

44   By 1906, though, women could vote in only four Western states: Colorado, Utah, Idaho, and Wyoming. "Could it be," some women wondered, "that success is impossible?"

45   After a long and active life, Susan died in 1906 at age 86. She had been right after all. Failure *was* impossible. Success just took a long time.

This stamp, issued in 1936, is one of two stamps honoring Susan B. Anthony.

46   It took 14 more years. In 1920, President Woodrow Wilson signed the 19th Amendment to the Constitution, giving women all over the nation the right to vote. No wonder the 19th Amendment is often called the Susan B. Anthony Amendment!

47   In recent years, this great fighter for women's rights has been remembered in many ways. The United States Post Office issued a Susan B. Anthony postage stamp. The United States Mint made a silver dollar bearing her image. If she were alive today, these honors would please her. But the continuing efforts of women to win full equality with men would surely please her most of all.

Working with Words

7. The word *contracts* (paragraph 6) means:
   (*a*) business letters   (*b*) unpaid bills
   (*c*) legal agreements   (*d*) birth certificates

8. The expression closest in meaning to *plodded* (paragraph 18) is:
   (*a*) stepped along quickly
   (*b*) walked slowly and heavily
   (*c*) skipped lightly
   (*d*) marched briskly

9. A *penalty* (paragraph 38) is a:
   (*a*) reward   (*b*) handwriting   (*c*) speech   (*d*) punishment

10. An *association* (paragraph 41) has:
    (*a*) members and goals
    (*b*) paragraphs and sentences
    (*c*) arms and legs
    (*d*) steps and doors

EXERCISES

Putting Events in Sequence

   A.   Write the letters of each set of events in the order in which the events happened in Susan B. Anthony's life. For example, would you answer #1 by writing *a-b* or *b-a*? If you need help, look back at the story.

1. *a.* During the Civil War, she works against slavery.
   b. She helps get a women's rights law passed in New York State.

2. *a.* With 15 other women, she votes in a national election.
   b. The 14th and 15th Amendments to the U.S. Constitution are passed.

3. *a.* She begins to work for an amendment to give American women the vote.
   b. She is arrested for voting.

4. *a.* Judge Hunt declares her guilty.
   b. She becomes president of the National American Woman Suffrage Association.

5. *a.* A postage stamp and a silver dollar honor her.
   b. The 19th Amendment, giving American women the vote, is passed.

Making Inferences

B.   Use what you have read about Susan B. Anthony to infer, or figure out, the correct choice.

1. Susan's belief in equal rights for women was shared by:
   (*a*) all women   (*b*) no women
   (*c*) some New Yorkers   (*d*) all New Yorkers

2. Susan was born in (*Hint:* See paragraph 45.):
   (*a*) 1800   (*b*) 1820   (*c*) 1850   (*d*) 1873

3. In Susan's time, the newspapers viewed women's rights with:
   (*a*) sympathy   (*b*) indifference   (*c*) anger   (*d*) curiosity

4. Today, Susan would regard a national Equal Rights Amendment as:
   (*a*) dangerous   (*b*) good   (*c*) unnecessary   (*d*) foolish

Understanding Cause and Effect

C.   Write the letter of the best choice.

1. The real effect of Susan's trial by the U.S. government was to:
   (*a*) make her pay a fine
   (*b*) prove Judge Hunt was right
   (*c*) win greater support for women's rights
   (*d*) hurt the cause of women's suffrage

2. The 19th Amendment is often called the Susan B. Anthony Amendment because:
   (*a*) she wrote it with President Wilson
   (*b*) she signed it at the White House
   (*c*) she lived to see it passed
   (*d*) she worked hard for it

3. Susan wanted women to be able to vote because they would then be able to:
   (*a*) change the laws
   (*b*) obey the laws
   (*c*) understand the laws
   (*d*) ignore the laws

4. When women were finally able to vote, the effect was to:
   (*a*) give men more power
   (*b*) give husbands more power
   (*c*) give women greater power than men
   (*d*) give women more power

Separating Fact from Opinion

   D.   Tell which is a *fact* and which is an *opinion*.

1. Susan was a brave woman.

2. She helped women win the right to vote.

3. She was put on trial for voting.

4. She should never have been put on trial.

Choosing the Best Title

   E.   Write the number of the best title for the story of Susan B. Anthony.

1. A Pioneer for Women's Rights

2. The Susan B. Anthony Silver Dollar

3. The Trial of Susan B. Anthony

4. Women's Rights Today

Speaking, Listening, and Writing

   F.   Be prepared to discuss one of the following topics with your classmates.

1. Why do you think so many people—women as well as men— were against giving women the right to vote?

2. Today, some people believe that women who stay home to keep house and raise their children are working at a job. Such women, it is said, should be paid wages like any other worker. How do you feel about this idea? Why?

G.   Write a paragraph or more about one of the following topics.

1. Tell what problems Susan faced when she collected names for a petition on women's rights in New York State.

2. What do you think were some of the personal qualities that helped Susan in her work for women's rights?

3. Write a brief letter to Susan telling her about some of the rights women have today but didn't have in her time.

A famous dancer makes some hard choices.

6. *Maria Tallchief*

Part I

1   **As the lights in the theater** grow dim, the audience becomes still. These people are about to see the *Firebird* ballet, starring the American dancer Maria Tallchief.

2   With a great leap, Maria Tallchief, dressed as the Firebird, seems to fly onto the stage. She is tall and beautiful. A spinning golden light shows her bare arms and shoulders glittering with gold dust. She wears a bright red costume. A long red feather rises from a small golden crown on her head.

3   The Firebird is a magical being, both woman and bird. Her dance of graceful high leaps across the stage looks like a bird in flight. The music plays even faster, and the golden light on the Firebird turns more quickly. High on the tips of her toes, the lovely dancer spins swiftly across the stage.

4   The Firebird turns and leaps to the side of the stage, out of sight. As the curtain falls, the first part of the ballet ends.

5   The people in the audience clap wildly. Some even stand up and cheer. On this evening of November 27, 1949, they have just seen Maria Tallchief dance for the first time in her most famous role.

6   Like all great dancers, Maria Tallchief made even the most difficult leaps and turns seem easy. But behind

her ease and grace were years of hard work. Behind
every move Maria Tallchief made on the stage stretched
a lifetime of training and practice.

7   Maria Tallchief was born in 1925 in Fairfax, Okla-

homa, on the Osage Indian reservation. Her parents named her Elizabeth Marie Tallchief, but her family called her Betty Marie. Her mother was of Scottish-Irish background. Her father was Alexander Tallchief, an Osage Indian.

8   The Osages were better off than most other Native Americans. Oil had been found on the Osage reservation, and the tribe had been paid large sums of money for the oil. With his share of the money, Mr. Tallchief bought real estate. The Tallchief family was able to live comfortably.

9   At an early age, Betty Marie showed that she was talented. When she was only three years old, she could already play tunes on the piano. She learned music quickly and well.

10   Mrs. Tallchief had high hopes for Betty Marie. She dreamed that some day her daughter would become a famous concert pianist. A strict mother, she made Betty Marie work hard at her music lessons.

11   Mrs. Tallchief also wanted her daughter to learn how to dance. When Betty Marie was only four years old, she began to take ballet lessons.

12   Betty Marie was really too young for ballet. Most children do not begin to learn ballet until they are seven or eight years old. Her teacher soon taught her to dance on the tips of her toes. Ballet teachers usually do not let their students toe dance until the students have had one to three years of special training.

13   Betty Marie was lucky that she had a strong young body. Otherwise, these very early ballet lessons might have hurt her badly.

14   "We should move to a big city," Mrs. Tallchief said to her husband one day. "Betty Marie could get better training in music and dance in a big city."

15   "That sounds like a good idea," Mr. Tallchief agreed. So when Betty Marie was eight, the family moved to Los Angeles, California.

Finding Details

1. This part of the story describes Maria Tallchief dancing in a
   ballet. How carefully did you read? Write the number of the
   paragraph in which you are told:
   a. how she was dressed
   b. the name of the ballet
   c. when the ballet took place
   d. what the Firebird is

2. You learn about Maria Tallchief's family background in paragraphs:
   (*a*) 7 and 8   (*b*) 9 and 10   (*c*) 11 and 12   (*d*) 13 and 14

Part II

16   **In Los Angeles,** Betty Marie went to public school
and did well there. The most important things in her
life, however, were her piano and ballet lessons.

17   Her new ballet teacher, Ernest Belcher, saw that
Betty Marie had talent. But he also knew that she had
been taught to do too much too soon—and it was all
wrong.

18   "You'll have to start all over again," he told her.
"Your body needs to be trained the right way."

19   For two hours every day, Betty Marie studied ballet
all over again from the very beginning. It was slow, hard
work. Each day, she faced the wall in Ernest Belcher's
studio. With both her hands on the wooden bar, she
practiced each of the five basic positions of ballet, month
after month.

20   "Watch your posture," Mr. Belcher would say to her.
"Shoulders down—back straight."

21   Later her teacher taught her to bend her knees in each of the basic positions. She practiced this for months. Slowly Betty Marie went over and over all the basic movements the ballet dancer must learn.

22   Mrs. Tallchief still wanted her daughter to become a concert pianist. So in addition to daily ballet lessons, Betty Marie also practiced the piano for several hours every day.

23   Betty Marie did not mind all this hard work. On her twelfth birthday, she gave a concert, first playing the piano, then dancing for her audience. Although she loved both music and dance, she could not become a professional performer in both. She had to choose between piano and ballet.

24   By the time she was in high school, she got a leading part in a ballet. Betty Marie, who was then 15, danced before a large audience in the big Hollywood Bowl. Afterward, the newspapers praised her. She had indeed danced beautifully. She had felt new power and freedom in her body.

25   "This is what I really want to do," she told herself. "I'll have to give up playing the piano. I want to spend all my time dancing."

Writing Details

3. Write the missing details in each of the following.
   a. Each day, Betty Marie studied ballet for _____ hours.
   b. On her twelfth birthday, she performed by _____ and _____.
   c. When she was 15, she danced in the big _____ before a large audience.

4. Write a complete sentence telling:
   a. what two things Betty Marie did after school each day
   b. what two choices were open to her
   c. what choice she made

Part III

26   **The best ballet teachers** and the best ballet companies were in New York City. After Betty Marie finished high school, her parents let her go there. She was then 17 years old. In New York, she looked up Serge Denham, the director of the Ballet Russe de Monte Carlo. He had seen her dance in California.

27   "I remember you," he told her. "I think you are a gifted young dancer. I would like to try you out in my company."

28   As the newest dancer in the ballet company, Betty Marie had a hard time. The other girls treated her badly. The young dancers were always afraid that somebody else would get a part in a ballet before they did. She wrote to her mother back in California, "They do not like me, through no fault of mine."

29   Betty Marie learned that the life of a professional dancer is not easy. Each morning, she practiced for several hours. Each afternoon, she rehearsed with the other dancers. In the evenings, she stood offstage and watched the company's regular dancers perform.

30   Gradually, she began to get small parts. One evening, she had to dance three different parts in the same ballet. In another ballet, *Rodeo*, she had only a walk-on part. But her acting was so good that even Mr. Denham noticed her.

31   In those days, the most famous ballet dancers were Russian. American dancers were expected to take Russian names.

32   "I'll change my first name to Maria," Betty Marie said to Mr. Denham. "But I want to keep the name Tallchief. I'm proud of my Indian background."

33   The director of the Ballet Russe did not object. "Anyone can put on a Russian name," he said. "But not

many young women can dance like you, Maria Tall-chief."

34   Mr. Denham was not the only one who admired her grace and power as a dancer. Another man who watched her with great interest was the famous choreographer George Balanchine. (A choreographer is a person who makes up dances.)

35   Mr. Balanchine created fine ballets for the Ballet Russe. He worked out the steps and the movements for all the dancers in the company. He was also an experienced dancer and an excellent teacher.

36   He began to work closely with Maria. Like her mother, he believed that the talented and beautiful young ballerina had a bright future. (A ballerina is a female ballet dancer.) Under his patient training, her dancing steadily improved.

37   In 1946, Maria and George Balanchine were married. Soon afterward, they both left the Ballet Russe de Monte Carlo. Maria had been with the company for five years. From then on, the careers of Maria Tallchief and George Balanchine were linked closely together.

Finding the Main Idea

5. The main idea of paragraph 29 is best expressed by sentence:
   (a) 1   (b) 2   (c) 3   (d) 4

6. Which of the following sentences best expresses the main idea of paragraphs 34–37?
   (a) George Balanchine was a famous choreographer.
   (b) Maria Tallchief and George Balanchine got married.
   (c) George Balanchine had an important effect on Maria's career.
   (d) Maria left the Ballet Russe de Monte Carlo.

Part IV

38   **For a number of years,** Maria was the leading dancer for the New York City Ballet Company. George Balanchine created many dances just for her. His training and her talent made her one of America's greatest ballerinas.

39   Along with the applause of audiences, Maria received many honors and awards. She enjoyed them all and worked even harder at her dancing. But she felt that something was missing from her life. She also wanted to have a child.

40   George Balanchine did not want to have children. The ballet was his whole life. It seemed to him that the ballet should be Maria's whole life, too.

41   After a number of years, Maria's marriage to George Balanchine ended. She continued to work with him, however, and to dance with the New York City Ballet Company. She was still one of its finest dancers.

42   In 1957, she married Henry Paschen, Jr., a general contractor, or builder, from Chicago. After three years of marriage, they had a baby girl, Elise Maria.

43   The next several years were difficult ones for Maria. As a young girl, she had been torn between two loves— piano and the ballet. Now she was torn between two other loves—the ballet and her family.

44   Her work as a dancer often kept her far away from her husband and her daughter. Mr. Paschen, who worked in Chicago, was proud of his wife. But he and Elise Maria missed her as much as she missed them.

45   When Maria was 41 years old, she felt it was time to make the hardest decision of all. She always gave herself fully to whatever she did. She had turned from the piano to give herself fully to the ballet. Now she decided to give herself fully to family life.

46   In 1966, she ended her career of 24 years as a ballet dancer. Returning to Chicago, she took up her new career as Maria Tallchief—homemaker.

47   However, in 1974, when her daughter Elise Maria was in college, Maria returned to the world of ballet. In 1974, she started a ballet school, and, in 1980, she founded the Chicago City Ballet. As co-artistic director of this company, she continues the fine tradition of ballet that George Balanchine taught and that she made famous.

Working with Words

7. The word that is LEAST like *glittering* (paragraph 2) is:
   (*a*) flashing   (*b*) shining   (*c*) shouting   (*d*) sparkling

8. A *reservation* (paragraph 7) is a piece of land that has been:
   (*a*) set aside for a special purpose
   (*b*) kept open for all to use
   (*c*) flooded by water from a reservoir
   (*d*) planted with a different crop each year

9. Use the following list of related words to write the missing words below.

   performer (paragraph 23)
   performing
   performance
   perform

   a. Betty Marie was chosen to _____ in a ballet.
   b. She was the star _____ in this dance.
   c. The newspapers praised her _____.
   d. During the years with Balanchine, she was constantly _____ ballets he created for her.

10. A *director* (paragraph 26) is most like a:
    (*a*) student   (*b*) dancer   (*c*) manager   (*d*) follower

EXERCISES

Putting Events in Sequence

A. Write the letters of each set of events in the order in which the events happened in Maria Tallchief's life. For example, would you answer #1 by writing *a-b* or *b-a*? If you need help, look back at the story.

1. *a.* The Tallchief family moves to California.
   b. Betty Marie begins to take ballet and piano lessons.

2. *a.* Betty Marie chooses dancing and gives up playing the piano.
   b. She goes to New York City.

3. *a.* She changes her name to Maria Tallchief.
   b. She studies ballet with Ernest Belcher.

4. *a.* She meets Serge Denham.
   b. She marries George Balanchine.

5. *a.* She remarries and has a baby girl.
   b. She decides to give up dancing.

Making Inferences

B. Use what you have read about Maria Tallchief to infer, or figure out, the correct choice.

1. You can infer that most children do not begin to learn ballet until they are seven or eight years old because:
   (*a*) they are not tall enough until then
   (*b*) their bodies are not strong enough until then
   (*c*) the lessons would interfere with their schoolwork
   (*d*) it is against the law

2. Which of the following is a direct statement, NOT an inference?
   (*a*) Maria's second ballet teacher was a better teacher than her first one.
   (*b*) Maria was an obedient daughter.

(*c*) Maria began her ballet career in New York City.

(*d*) Although George Balanchine and Maria were divorced, they continued to respect each other's abilities.

3. The major decisions in Maria's life involved her:
(*a*) mother   (*b*) father
(*c*) American Indian heritage   (*d*) career

4. It seems reasonable to infer that Maria works today chiefly as a:
(*a*) dancer   (*b*) choreographer   (*c*) pianist   (*d*) teacher

Understanding Cause and Effect

C.   Write the letter of the correct choice.

1. At her mother's insistence, Maria:
(*a*) studied both music and dance
(*b*) dropped out of school
(*c*) moved to Chicago
(*d*) changed her first name to Maria

2. Maria moved to New York City because:
(*a*) her husband worked there
(*b*) the best ballet teachers and companies were there
(*c*) she disliked California
(*d*) her mother told her to go there

3. As a professional ballerina, Maria kept the name Tallchief because:
(*a*) she did what her mother wanted
(*b*) she liked the way it sounded
(*c*) she had no other choice
(*d*) she was proud of her Native American background

4. Maria gave up dancing because she wanted to devote herself to:
(*a*) the piano   (*b*) her family
(*c*) making more money   (*d*) teaching ballet

Separating Fact from Opinion

   D.   Tell which is a *fact* and which is an *opinion*.

1. Maria ought not to have studied both piano and ballet.

2. Maria was the greatest ballerina of her time.

3. Twice in her life, Maria had to make important choices.

4. In both cases, she made the right choice.

Choosing the Best Title

   E.   Write the number of the best title for the story of Maria Tallchief.

1. The Osage Indians

2. Maria Tallchief and George Balanchine

3. The Ballet Russe de Monte Carlo

4. The Making of a Ballerina

Speaking, Listening, and Writing

   F.   **Dictation:** With your book closed and a sheet of paper and a pen or pencil for taking notes, listen while your teacher reads aloud a brief passage from the story of Maria Tallchief. Then answer the questions your teacher asks.

(*Note:* The questions appear in a separate Answer Key.)

   G.   Write a paragraph or more about one of the following topics.

1. How was George Balanchine important in Maria's life?

2. How did Maria's mother help her daughter's career?

3. Tell about someone you know or know about who worked hard to accomplish something. (You may wish to make up a name for the real person you choose to write about.)

With a knife, a gun, and a prayer, a brave woman works on the Underground Railroad.

7. Harriet Tubman

Part I

1   **Harriet Tubman was born** about 1820 on a big farm in eastern Maryland. Early in her life, she learned the two most important facts about herself: She was black and she was a slave. As she grew up, she found out what being an enslaved person meant.

2   Like many slaves in the Old South, Harriet was beaten often. She was hit for not being fast enough at her work. For taking a lump of sugar out of her mistress' sugar bowl, she was whipped long and hard. Sometimes she was beaten simply because her master or mistress was in a bad mood.

3   When Harriet was in her early teens, she received a serious injury. She was working in the field one evening. One of the slaves, a young man, left the field to go to the village store without telling anyone. The white overseer (boss) followed him, and Harriet followed the overseer.

4   In the store, the overseer swore that he would whip the young man for leaving his work. As the overseer reached for his whip, the young man dashed out the door.

5   "Stop him!" the overseer yelled to Harriet. "Help me catch him and tie him up."

6   Instead, Harriet planted herself in the doorway. She blocked the overseer from running after the young man.

7   In a rage, the overseer grabbed a two-pound iron weight. He threw it with all his might at the running youth. The weight struck Harriet on her forehead. With a little moan, she dropped to the ground.

8   Nobody expected Harriet to live. It took many months before she recovered from that terrible blow. For the rest of her life, she carried a big scar on her forehead. The blow to her head also gave Harriet strange "blackouts." She would suddenly seem to fall asleep for a few minutes. This could happen to her anywhere, any time.

9   Like other slaves, Harriet was not allowed to go to school. It was illegal for slaves to learn to read and write. But her father, Benjamin, taught her well what she would need to know in later years.

10   From her father, Harriet learned to find the North Star in the sky. "Just keep that star ahead of you," Benjamin told her, "and you'll always know you're heading north."

11   From her father, Harriet also learned other ways to find her way in the woods. "On a cloudy night, when

you can't find the North Star," Benjamin told her, "feel for the moss on the trees. Moss always grows on the north side of a tree."

12   Benjamin showed her how to move silently in the woods. He taught her which nuts and berries she could eat. He told her how to cover her trail by wading up a stream or river. "No bloodhound can follow a trail in running water," he reminded her.

Finding Details

1. Give the number of the paragraph that answers each question.
    a. Where was Harriet born?
    b. About how old was Harriet when she was seriously injured?
    c. What were the two permanent results of this injury?
    d. Were slaves allowed to go to school?

2. This part of the story mentions three things that Harriet learned from her father. Give the numbers of the paragraphs that tell these details.

Part II

13   **Harriet was only five** feet tall when she grew up, but she was stronger than most men. She could lift heavy barrels like a man. She could even pull a loaded wagon like an ox. When visitors came to the farm, they were taken to see Harriet work.

14   Harriet decided to try to save enough money to buy herself from her master. In the daytime, she plowed fields or chopped wood. At night, she scrubbed floors, took in washing, or hired herself out to work in a kitchen. Sometimes she could hardly lift her tired, aching body. But she kept on working. Slowly, she was saving money to buy her freedom.

15   By the end of a year, she had saved 20 dollars. She went to see the master. How much money did he want, she asked, to set her free? The master roared with laughter. It seemed to him like a great joke.

16   "How much money?" he repeated. "Five hundred dollars. That's how much. You bring me $500, and I'll let you go."

17   Harriet left feeling sick at heart. Would she live long enough to make that much money? She doubted it. But she kept on working and saving money for her freedom anyway.

18   In 1849, Harriet's owner suddenly died. His death frightened her because now she could no longer hope to buy her freedom. But something even worse could happen. Harriet was afraid that she would be sold to the cotton planters deeper in the South.

19   "I'll run away," she told herself. "I have to go before it's too late."

20   Harriet had often heard about the Quakers. These people, who dressed in plain black or gray clothing, were also called Friends. A gentle Christian folk who hated slavery, they were truly friends to black people.

21   From a Quaker woman in a nearby town, Harriet learned about another Quaker—a shoemaker named Thomas Garrett. He lived farther north in Wilmington, Delaware. Although Delaware was also a slave state, Garrett was active in the Underground Railroad.

22   This was not a real railroad, and it was not really underground. It was actually a group of brave men and women—both black and white—who helped slaves escape north to freedom. Members of the Underground Railroad hid fugitive slaves in their homes and shops. They fed the runaways, clothed them, and guided them along to the next "station" on their trip north.

23   The Quaker woman told Harriet how to travel to Delaware. Next to Delaware, she told her, was the state of Pennsylvania, which had no slavery. There Harriet would be free.

24   Back in her cabin, Harriet prepared for her escape. Into her cloth bag, she put a week's supply of food, a few coins, and a sharp hunting knife.

25   "There is one of two things I have a right to," she told herself, "freedom or death. If I can't have one, I'll have the other. But no man will ever take me alive."

Writing Details

3. Write the missing name or names in each of the following sentences.
   a. _____ told Harriet she could be free for $500.
   b. The gentle Christians who opposed slavery were known as _____ or _____.
   c. The organization that helped slaves escape to freedom was called the _____.
   d. From her home in Maryland, Harriet planned to travel to _____ and then to _____.

4. To make money to buy her freedom, Harriet worked at several different jobs. Mention four kinds of work she did.

Part III

26   **That night Harriet** slipped away into the woods. A long and dangerous journey lay ahead of her. But as she walked, she kept her eye on the North Star. It pointed the way to freedom.

27   It took Harriet six days to reach Wilmington, Delaware. There, Thomas Garrett concealed her in a secret little room above his shoe shop. Early in the morning, she walked alone to the border between Delaware and Pennsylvania. A wooden signpost marked the border. With a beating heart, she stepped across the line from slavery to freedom.

28   In later years, Harriet described how she felt at that moment: "When I found I had crossed that line, I looked at my hands to see if I was the same person. There was such a glory over everything. The sun came like gold through the trees and over the fields. I felt like I was in heaven."

29   For a time, Harriet lived in the city of Philadelphia. One of the first things she bought for herself there was a long-barreled pistol. It was not enough for her that she had won her own freedom. She wanted to help her family and other black people to be free.

30   In Philadelphia, Harriet became a friend of William Still, the secretary of the Pennsylvania Anti-Slavery Society. He told her all about the work of the Underground Railroad. As Harriet listened to William Still talk, her eyes glowed.

31   "I want to work on the Underground Railroad, too," she said. "I want to go back down South and lead my people out of slavery—the way Moses led his people out of slavery in the Bible."

32   William Still frowned and shook his head.

33   "As soon as you go back," he warned her, "you'll be considered a slave again. If they catch you, they will sell you back into slavery. Or they might shoot you."

34   "They won't catch me so easily," Harriet said with a grim smile. She thought of the sharp hunting knife and the pistol hidden in her cloth bag.

35   William Still looked at her dark, strong face. "Yes," he said softly, "I believe you."

Finding the Main Idea

5. The main idea of paragraph 28 is:
   (a) Harriet crossed a state line.
   (b) She noticed how beautiful the sun looked that morning.
   (c) She felt great joy at being free.
   (d) She saw a signpost that she couldn't read.

6. The main idea of paragraphs 29–35 is:
   (*a*) Harriet built a life for herself in Philadelphia.
   (*b*) She decided to help free other slaves.
   (*c*) She became friends with William Still.
   (*d*) She purchased a gun.

Part IV

36   **After only one year** of freedom, Harriet returned to Maryland. In her cloth bag, she kept her hunting knife. Strapped to her leg, under her skirts, was the long-barreled pistol.

37   She made her way alone through great dangers. She led her sister Mary Ann, her sister's husband, and their two children north to Philadelphia and freedom. A few months after that, she slipped back into Maryland to free her oldest brother, James, and two of his friends. Later she was also able to free her parents.

38   In 1850, the United States Congress passed the Fugitive Slave Law. The new law said that all slaves who had run away must be returned to their masters. From then on, Harriet could not leave escaped slaves in the North. It was no longer a safe place for them.

39   "I can't trust Uncle Sam with my people any more," she said. "Now I have to take them clear up to Canada."

40   For about 10 years before the Civil War, she made 19 trips into the South. She helped over 300 men, women, and children escape. She led them along the perilous road to freedom all the way to Canada. To her people, she was like a second Moses, and they called her by that name.

41   Slaveholders in Delaware, Maryland, and Virginia hated her. She was stealing slaves, and slaves were their property! They put up posters offering a reward of $40,000 for anyone who caught Harriet.

42   Once, when she was in the South, she had one of her brief "blackouts." Luckily, her friends found her sitting on a park bench. She was fast asleep right under a poster that read: WANTED! HARRIET TUBMAN— DEAD OR ALIVE!

43   When the Civil War began, she talked to black men about joining the Union Army and fighting for the North. She also served as a nurse with these black soldiers.

44   Since nobody knew the secret ways in and out of the South as well as Harriet, she became a scout for the Union forces. In 1863, she led three Union gunboats in a bold raid into South Carolina. They brought back with them 756 freed slaves. On other raids, with Harriet serving as the scout, thousands more slaves were set free.

45   After the Civil War, she settled with her parents in Auburn, New York. Black people who remembered "Moses" came looking for her. Some who were homeless stayed to live with her. She took care of them all by selling fruits and vegetables in the streets of Auburn.

46   Although she was old and poor, Harriet still wanted to help her people. She dreamed of building a home for poor, homeless black women and men. After years of asking for help and working for her dream, she finally succeeded. In 1908, the town of Auburn built the Harriet Tubman Home in her honor.

47   On March 10, 1913, at the age of 93, Harriet died. In her memory, the people of Auburn put up a small bronze sign. On it were written Harriet Tubman's proudest words: "On my Underground Railroad, I never ran my train off the track and I never lost a passenger."

Working with Words

7. Something *illegal* (paragraph 9) is:
    (*a*) sick
    (*b*) not necessary
    (*c*) impossible to understand
    (*d*) against the law

8. A *fugitive* person (paragraph 22) is most likely to be:
    (*a*) hunted   (*b*) ignored   (*c*) paid well   (*d*) doubted

9. The word *concealed* (paragraph 27) means:
    (*a*) shown   (*b*) hidden   (*c*) invited   (*d*) canceled

10. A *perilous* road (paragraph 40) is full of:
    (*a*) pebbles   (*b*) people   (*c*) dangers   (*d*) surprises

EXERCISES

Putting Events in Sequence

A. Write the letters of each set of events in the order in which the events happened in Harriet Tubman's life. For example, would you answer #1 by writing *a-b* or *b-a*? If you need help, look back at the story.

1. *a.* Harriet Tubman develops strange "blackouts."
   b. An overseer hits her with a two-pound iron weight.

2. *a.* Her master dies.
   b. The Quakers help her escape.

3. *a.* She goes to live in Philadelphia.
   b. She begins to work for the Underground Railroad.

4. *a.* She serves as a nurse during the Civil War.
   b. She returns to the South and frees her family.

5. *a.* She becomes a scout for the Union forces.
   b. She moves to Auburn, New York.

Making Inferences

B. Use what you have read about Harriet Tubman to infer, or figure out, the correct choice.

1. It seems safe to infer that Harriet's father expected his daughter to:
   (*a*) marry and have children
   (*b*) buy herself out of slavery
   (*c*) escape from slavery
   (*d*) help free other slaves

2. Being sold to the cotton planters deeper in the South would make escape from slavery:
   (*a*) easier   (*b*) harder   (*c*) unnecessary   (*d*) undesirable

3. In helping slaves escape to the North, the Quakers were:
 (*a*) obeying the law
 (*b*) making money
 (*c*) taking great risks
 (*d*) gaining slaves for themselves

4. You can infer that the people of Auburn, New York, thought of Harriet with:
 (*a*) scorn   (*b*) amusement   (*c*) anger   (*d*) admiration

Understanding Cause and Effect

  C.   Write the letter of the correct choice.

1. Because she was a slave, Harriet was:
 (*a*) sent abroad   (*b*) put in prison   (*c*) beaten   (*d*) educated

2. The death of her master caused Harriet to:
 (*a*) rejoice
 (*b*) worry
 (*c*) work harder
 (*d*) buy her freedom sooner

3. The chief effect of Harriet's many trips into the South was to:
 (*a*) bring on the Civil War
 (*b*) free many slaves
 (*c*) satisfy slaveholders
 (*d*) repeal, or cancel, the Fugitive Slave Law

4. During the Civil War, Harriet served as a scout because:
 (*a*) she was a strong woman
 (*b*) she was short enough to hide easily
 (*c*) she had both a gun and a knife
 (*d*) she knew secret ways in and out of the South

Separating Fact from Opinion

  D.   Tell which is a *fact* and which is an *opinion*.

1. Harriet was born before the Civil War.

2. She was as great a leader as Moses.

3. The Fugitive Slave Law was passed in 1850.

4. It was not a fair law.

Choosing the Best Title

E. Write the number of the best title for the story of Harriet Tubman.

1. Runaway Slave

2. The "Moses" of Her People

3. The Union Scout

4. The Underground Railroad

Speaking, Listening, and Writing

F. Be prepared to discuss one of the following topics with your classmates.

1. Why was "Moses" a good name for Harriet Tubman?

2. What do you think was her bravest deed?

G. Write a paragraph or more about one of the following topics. (If you wish, you may make up a name for the real person you will write about.)

1. What were some of the things Harriet Tubman did to help others?

2. Tell about somebody you know or know about who struggled hard to help others.

3. Tell about somebody you know or know about who had a hard life and tried to change it.

A lover of freedom gives his life to help the American Revolution.

8. Haym Salomon

Part I

1   **You probably know** some of the great names of the American Revolution: Benjamin Franklin, Thomas Jefferson, George Washington. One more name must be added—Haym Salomon. Who was this man? What did he have to do with the American Revolution?

2   Haym was born about 1740 to a Jewish family in Poland. He grew up a quiet, thoughtful person, more of a listener than a talker. He could pick up new languages the way a sponge soaks up water. In time, he learned nine languages: Polish, Hebrew, Russian, German, Dutch, Spanish, Italian, French, and English. Despite his peaceful ways, however, he soon found himself fighting in a war for freedom.

3   When Haym was still a young man, Russia attacked Poland. With his native land in great peril, he quickly joined the struggle. He fought against the Russians with Poland's two great leaders, Casimir Pulaski and Thaddeus Kosciusko. Although the Polish people and their leaders fought bravely, the Russians won. Haym had to flee, first to England and then, in 1772, to America.

4   In New York City, Haym worked for the merchants who bought and sold goods from the ships that sailed out of the busy city. He worked hard and saved his

money. Soon he was able to open his own office. Because he spoke many languages, had great business talent, and was honest in his dealings, he became one of the most successful and respected businessmen of the city.

5   In his daily work, Haym met many people. Among them was a man from Scotland named Alexander MacDougall. The two soon became close friends.

6   They could not have been more different. Haym was a small, thin man with soft brown eyes and a gentle manner. Alexander had a strong body, sharp blue eyes, and rough and ready ways.

7   In spite of their differences, the two friends were alike in one important way. They shared a burning love of freedom.

8   "There's a great fight coming," Alexander said one afternoon as he sat in his friend's office. "When it comes, New York will be in the middle of it."

9   "What fight is this?" Haym asked.

10   The Scotsman threw back his head and laughed. "Just look about you, man. On the other side of the ocean in England sits King George III. He spends his days thinking up new taxes for us to pay. At night, he dreams of new ways to trouble us. And what rights do we have? New York is only a colony. We belong to England the same as the other 12 colonies. But we can do something, Haym. We *will* do something!"

11   "Who is this 'we' you talk of?" asked Haym.

12   "The Sons of Liberty."

13   "And who, if you please, are these Sons of Liberty?"

14   Alexander leaned forward and lowered his voice. "We are men who want to be our own masters. We have joined together to fight for freedom."

15   Haym smiled at his friend. "I see," he said. "I have left one fight in Poland only to find another one in

America. But I am not sorry. Freedom is a rare and precious thing. I will join your Sons of Liberty."

Finding Details

1. Give the number of the paragraph or paragraphs in which you learn:
   a. why Haym had to flee from Poland
   b. which languages he could speak
   c. how Haym and Alexander were different and how they were alike
   d. who the Sons of Liberty were

2. In this part of the story, you are told three reasons for Haym's success as a businessman. Which paragraph tells these reasons?

Part II

16   **During the next few years,** Haym worked with his friend Alexander and the Sons of Liberty. At the same time, England and its American colonies moved toward war.

17   On July 4, 1776, the Americans declared that they were a new nation, independent from England. Two months later, a large British army took over New York City.

18   On the evening of September 22, 1776, Haym was sitting at home. Suddenly, a pounding on his front door shook the house.

19   "Yes? What is it?" he asked, opening the door. A line of red-coated British soldiers stood outside.

20   "Haym Salomon!" the officer in charge cried. "You are under arrest for working against the King."

21   The soldiers marched Haym off to a large building in which American prisoners were kept. This old building had no roof. The heavy rains of September and October poured down on the Americans. Some of them died in that prison.

22   Day after day, Haym sat, soaking wet and chilled to the bone. He began to cough. For the rest of his life, his lungs were weak, and he was a sick man. Perhaps he, too, would have died in prison if his talent for languages hadn't saved him.

23   Almost 30,000 hired soldiers from Germany were fighting for England. They were called Hessians. Since the British officers spoke only English and the Hessians spoke only German, the British were unable to give orders to the Hessians. When the British learned that Haym spoke German, they were delighted. He could tell the Hessian soldiers what the British officers ordered. So the British let him out of prison.

24   For almost two years, Haym led a double life. The British used him to speak German for them. Although they tried to keep an eye on him, there was a lot about Haym they didn't know.

25   Whenever he spoke to the Hessian soldiers, he tried to win them over to the American side. Often he succeeded.

26   His house became a hiding place for wounded American soldiers. Haym even carried some of these wounded soldiers, concealed in his own wagon, past the British troops to the American army north of the city.

27   As a businessman, Haym traded with ships from many different places. Sometimes he learned about secret British plans. His work as a spy was very useful to General George Washington and his army.

28   Working secretly for the American Revolution, Haym risked his life day after day. His luck could not last forever. Some day the British would find out.

Writing Details

3. Write the month and year in which:
   a. the Americans declared their independence from England

    b. a large British army took over New York City (*Hint:* You must figure out this date.)

    c. Haym was arrested

4. Write two things the British did NOT know about Haym after they had let him out of prison.

Part III

29   **It happened one evening** in August 1778. A dozen British soldiers marched up to Haym's house. There was a knock on the door like thunder. He was taken from his house and placed under arrest again. This time the British said he was a spy. In wartime, spies were shot or hanged.

30   About a week later, Haym sat alone at night in his prison cell. At sunrise, he was to be hanged. Looking around at the dark walls of the little cell, he realized that he had only his wits to save him.

31   A young guard appeared at the cell door and spoke a few words in German. A Hessian! Perhaps this was Haym's chance.

32   "Good evening, friend," Haym said softly in German. "How do you like being a soldier?"

33   "Ach! It is no work for me," the Hessian answered. "Back home I was a farmer."

34   "And did you own your own farm?"

35   The young man sighed. "No. I rented land from my lord. I never had enough money to buy my own land."

36   Haym smiled to himself. He knew that General Washington had offered 50 acres of land to any Hessian who would leave the British.

37   "You could own your own land here in America," he said. "If you will help me, I will tell you how. What

do you care about these fine British officers? What do they know about farms and good land?"

38   In a little while, Haym had persuaded the young Hessian guard to let him escape. He did not dare go near his house because he knew it would be watched. Instead, he made his way north on foot. British soldiers were everywhere, yet he slipped past them all.

39   Two days after he was supposed to have been hanged, Haym was safe with the American army. The Americans were camped in Dobbs Ferry, just north of New York City. And at their head was his old friend, now *Captain* Alexander MacDougall!

40   "Join us," Alexander said as he showed Haym Salomon around the camp. "For your past services, you could be an officer."

41   Haym didn't answer. Instead, he looked around him, taking in everything in his quick way. He saw American soldiers in dirty, ragged clothing. Many of the men had no uniforms. Their guns and other supplies looked worn and old. They had very little food.

42   On the men's faces, though, was a look of strength and pride. Haym remembered that look. He had seen it years before, shining on the faces of the brave Polish fighters for freedom.

43   But Haym had learned that bravery was not enough. It had not saved Poland. An army needed guns and bullets and food and warm uniforms and blankets for the winter months. All this took money.

44   "No, my friend," he said at last. He turned to look at Alexander. "Let other men be officers. I have my own skills. I will get money to win the war."

45   "Where will you go now?" Alexander asked.

46   "Philadelphia is back in American hands," Haym answered. "It is an important center of business. There I can work best for freedom."

47   The next day Haym crossed by ferryboat to the west side of the Hudson River. He walked most of the hundred and more miles down to Philadelphia.

Finding the Main Idea

5. Which of the following sentences best states the main idea of paragraphs 30–38?
   (*a*) Haym made a lasting friendship with his Hessian guard and helped him get his own farm.
   (*b*) He found out why the Hessian's life was so hard.
   (*c*) He made a promise he couldn't keep.
   (*d*) He used his wits and his knowledge of German to save his life.

6. In paragraphs 40–44, Haym realizes:
   (*a*) that the spirit of the American troops was broken
   (*b*) how he could best help the American cause
   (*c*) what made his friend Alexander such a good officer
   (*d*) why the Hessian soldiers needed land

Part IV

48   **Haym arrived in Philadelphia** alone, sick, and with almost no money. His house, his business, and almost all his money were in New York City. Since the British army still controlled New York City, he had to begin all over again.

49   Haym rented an office on the waterfront. He set to work doing what he knew best—making money by buying and selling. He never took foolish risks. He was always honest in his dealings. Yet he made money quickly. Soon people spoke of him as one of the rich men of Philadelphia.

50   Haym had been right. Bravery was not enough. The 13 states were fighting a war with no way to pay for it. Without money, the American Revolution was in trouble. Telling no one, he began to pour money into the fight for freedom.

51   He raised large sums of money for the American army. Sometimes he simply gave his own money. Money

for new uniforms. Money for food. Money for guns, bullets, blankets, tents, horses, wagons—all the things that keep an army going.

52 Often, he made loans to people. He knew that the money would probably never be returned. Indeed, none of it was, but Haym didn't care.

53 He helped men who became famous in American history. And he helped many men who served well, but died unknown. Wherever there was a need, there was Haym Salomon.

54 All the time, the need grew greater. As Haym worked harder than ever, the cough that had begun in the British prison grew worse. One day, he found that he was coughing up blood.

55 "You must work less and rest more," said a doctor. "You're a sick man. The way you are driving yourself, you'll soon be a dead man."

56 "I don't have time," Haym said softly. "There's still too much to do."

57 As his health grew worse, he knew that he was dying. Yet he had to raise more money—always more money to keep the American Revolution alive.

58 Nobody knows how much money Haym raised for his country. Nobody knows how much of his own money he contributed. Records have been destroyed. Letters have been lost. Some history books say that when the war was over, the new nation owed Haym more than half a million dollars. In those days, that was a huge sum of money.

59 The United States never repaid its debt to Haym. In 1785, at the age of 45, he died a poor man.

60 Other men had come from Europe to help the American Revolution. Kosciusko and Pulaski had come from Poland. Baron von Steuben had come from Germany. Lafayette had come from France. They fought on the field of battle and became famous heroes.

61 Haym Salomon fought for America in his own way. He gave everything: all his money, all his energy, and—finally—his own life.

Working with Words

7. Something *precious* (paragraph 15) is:
   (*a*) valuable   (*b*) worthless   (*c*) illegal   (*d*) free

8. Use the following list of related words to supply the missing words below.

   > declared (paragraph 17)
   > declare
   > declaring
   > declaration

   a. The Americans wrote a _____ of their independence from England.

   b. The British officer _____ loudly that Haym was under arrest.

   c. Haym went along with the soldiers, all the while _____ his innocence.

   d. He would _____ his loyalty to the British while he worked secretly for the Americans.

9. A person who has been *persuaded* (paragraph 38) would most likely:
   (*a*) resist   (*b*) die   (*c*) recover   (*d*) agree

10. The word that is LEAST like *contributed* (paragraph 58) is:
    (*a*) loaned   (*b*) took   (*c*) donated   (*d*) gave

EXERCISES

Putting Events in Sequence

   A.   Write the letters of each set of events in the order in which the events happened in Haym Salomon's life. For example, would you answer #1 by writing *a-b* or *b-a*? If you need help, look back at the story.

1. *a.* Haym fights for Polish freedom from Russia.
   b. He goes to live in America.

2. *a.* He joins the Sons of Liberty.
   b. He becomes friends with Alexander MacDougall.

3. *a.* He serves as an American spy.
   b. The British release him from prison.

4. *a.* He talks his way out of prison.
   b. He goes to Philadelphia.

5. *a.* He raises money for the American Revolution.
   b. His friend Alexander asks him to join the American army.

Making Inferences

B.   Use what you have learned about Haym Salomon to infer, or figure out, the correct choice.

1. You can reasonably infer that for most people today, the life of Haym Salomon is still:
   (*a*) unknown   (*b*) familiar
   (*c*) hard to believe   (*d*) the subject of gossip

2. A term that does NOT accurately describe Haym is:
   (*a*) quiet   (*b*) freedom-loving
   (*c*) cowardly   (*d*) hard-working

3. According to the story, Haym's life was saved twice because he spoke both:
   (*a*) Polish and English   (*b*) French and German
   (*c*) German and English   (*d*) English and Spanish

4. Haym succeeded in life chiefly by using his:
   (*a*) rich relatives   (*b*) physical strength
   (*c*) charm   (*d*) brains

Understanding Cause and Effect

C.   Write the letter of the best choice.

1. Haym became friends with Alexander MacDougall because:
   (*a*) they were business partners
   (*b*) the two men were different in many ways
   (*c*) they both loved freedom
   (*d*) Alexander had saved his life

2. Haym succeeded in business because of his:
- (*a*) gift with languages
- (*b*) business talent
- (*c*) honesty
- (*d*) all of these

3. One lifelong effect on Haym of his first stay in a British prison was:
- (*a*) mental illness
- (*b*) weak lungs
- (*c*) poor eyesight
- (*d*) the inability to walk

4. Haym moved to Philadelphia because it was:
- (*a*) controlled by the British
- (*b*) the center of military action
- (*c*) where his family lived
- (*d*) controlled by the Americans

Separating Fact from Opinion

D.   Tell which is a *fact* and which is an *opinion*.

1. Haym could speak nine languages.

2. Anyone who can speak several languages must be clever.

3. The United States should have paid the money it owed to Haym.

4. Even if the government had offered to repay Haym, he would have refused to take the money.

Choosing the Best Title

E.   Write the number of the best title for the story of Haym Salomon.

1. A Prisoner of the British

2. General Washington's Spy

3. A Little-Known Hero of the American Revolution

4. A Man of Many Languages

Speaking, Listening, and Writing

F.   Working with one or two of your classmates, prepare some notes for a brief talk on one of the following topics.

1. Who do you think is a greater hero—a soldier on the battlefield or a person like Haym Salomon? Explain your answer.

2. Tell about somebody you know or know about who helped others but who never got any reward or credit for that help. (You may wish to make up a name for the real person you choose to tell about.)

G.   Write a paragraph or more about one of the following topics.

1. Haym was proud of his Polish background. From what you have read in the story, can you tell why? Explain your answer.

2. In your own words, tell how Haym escaped from being hanged as a spy.

3. Imagine that Haym Salomon were alive today. Write an invitation to him to visit your class and explain how he helped the cause of the American Revolution.

Here is the man who created Mickey Mouse, Donald Duck, and many other cartoon characters.

9. Walt Disney

Part I

1   **Have you ever seen** a Walt Disney film? Read a Walt Disney storybook? Listened to a Walt Disney record? Looked through a Walt Disney comic book? Millions of people have. They have also visited Disneyland in California and Disney World in Florida. The name *Walt Disney* is everywhere.

2   But who was Walt Disney? His cartoon characters—Mickey Mouse, Donald Duck, and many others—are better known than the man who made them.

3   When Walt was 16, World War I was just ending. He signed up as a volunteer for the Red Cross Ambulance Corps. For almost a year, he drove trucks, cars, and ambulances in France. In his free time, he drew cartoons (funny line-drawings) of American soldiers. He sent a letter covered with cartoons to his high school magazine back home. He filled one drawing pad after another with cartoons and sketches of people and places in France.

4   By the time Walt returned to America, he had already decided to make his living as an artist. In Kansas City, and later in Chicago, he went to art school. He loved to draw. Most of all, he enjoyed drawing cartoons.

5   In 1920, he drew cartoons for the Kansas City Film Ad Company. Those were the days of silent movies. Besides the main film, many movie houses showed cartoon

advertisements for local stores. On this job, Walt learned
how to make animated cartoons.

6   To make his cartoon characters seem to move, Walt
drew many pictures of the same figure. Each picture was
just a little different from the one before. All the pictures were photographed with movie film. Then the film
was shown on a screen. The final result was a cartoon
that seemed animated, or alive.

7   While Walt was still working at the Kansas City Film Ad Company, he set up his own animated cartoon company. He called it Laugh-O-Gram Films. He continued to work at his daytime job, and drew the Laugh-O-Grams at night.

8   He never made much money from his short, silent, black-and-white cartoons. But with each new film, he learned more about making animated cartoons. He even filmed a live girl with a cartoon background and cartoon characters. This early combination of cartoons and live action became important in his work years later.

9   One day in the Laugh-O-Gram office, Walt caught a mouse. He kept it as a pet and named it Mortimer. Walt decided to tame Mortimer. He drew a large circle on a piece of paper. Every time Mortimer tried to run out of the circle, Walt tapped him on the nose with a pencil. Mortimer the mouse learned to sit inside the circle while Walt drew cartoons.

10   At 21 years of age, Walt felt frustrated because he wasn't getting anywhere. Day after day, he was caught in a circle of hard work and little money. It seemed to him that he was as stuck as Mortimer.

11   In the summer of 1923, Walt decided to try his luck in Hollywood, California. (Before going, he set Mortimer the mouse free.) With his older brother Roy, he started a small animated cartoon company. Walt did all the artwork, while Roy handled all the business matters.

12   A young woman named Lillian Bounds came to work in the studio. Her job was to apply ink and paint to the cartoons. Sometimes, when she worked late, Walt drove her home at night.

13   "I want to get married," Walt told her, "but not until I'm 25 years old and I've saved up $10,000."

14   As the two young people saw more of each other, they fell in love. In the spring of 1925, Roy got married. Walt was best man at the wedding. Not long afterward, Walt asked Lillian to marry him.

15   "What about the $10,000?" she said with a smile. "And you're not even 25 yet."

16   "I don't want to wait," Walt said. "Let's get married now. I'll be 25 and have $10,000 soon."

17   In 1925, Walt married Lillian Bounds. As he had promised, he became 25 years old soon enough. But earning the $10,000 took more time.

Finding Details

1. In which paragraph or paragraphs do you learn about:
   a. Walt's first job
   b. a pet mouse
   c. Walt's move to California
   d. two marriages

2. Which paragraph explains how an animated cartoon is made?

Part II

18   **Two years after his marriage,** Walt and his wife went on a business trip to New York City. His business there turned out badly. The company that bought his films wanted to pay him less than before. The future looked dark for the Disney film studio.

19   "What good is all my work?" he asked Lillian as they rode the train back to California. "Am I ever going to get out of this endless circle of hard work and no real success? Every time I seem to be getting somewhere, bad luck hits me on the nose."

20   Suddenly, he remembered his pet mouse, Mortimer.

21   "Hey! How about a mouse?" he said to himself. "A cartoon Mortimer mouse with big round ears and a long tail!"

22   Taking out a sketch pad and a pencil, Walt began drawing. He drew a black mouse with skinny arms and legs and a big head. He drew short pants with two big buttons in front.

23   "There," he said, showing the drawing to Lillian. "Mortimer Mouse. How do you like him?"

24   "He's cute," she said. "But Mortimer's no name for a mouse."

25   "Maybe you're right. I'll make some more drawings and try some other names."

26   By the time the train reached California, Walt had made dozens of drawings of his mouse. He had even found a better name—Mickey Mouse.

27   The Disney studio set to work at once. It began to make a series of short Mickey Mouse cartoons. Like all movies of that time, they were black and white, and they had no sound.

28   The addition of sound to movies in 1927 excited Walt. New ideas and new ways to make his work better always excited him. The first Mickey Mouse cartoon with sound was called *Steamboat Willie.* Walt himself supplied Mickey Mouse's high, squeaky voice. In the many Mickey Mouse cartoons that followed, the mouse's voice was always that of Walt Disney.

29   *Steamboat Willie,* first shown in the fall of 1928, was an instant success. Audiences enjoyed hearing the music and the mouse's voice. There were also lively sound effects—bells, whistles, horns, and other funny noises. Most of all, the audiences loved Mickey Mouse.

30   Before long, Mickey Mouse was not just a star. He was a superstar. People all over the world knew him. In Germany, he was called *Michael Maus.* In France, he was *Michel Souris.* To audiences in Spain, he was *Miguel Ratoncito.* The Japanese called him *Miki Kuchi.*

31   Soon there were Mickey Mouse comic strips and comic books. The mouse could also be seen on clothing, toys, and even candy bars. Most popular of all were

Mickey Mouse wristwatches. Everyone loved the little mouse.

32   Mickey Mouse's great fame caused a problem for Walt. If the little mouse didn't behave himself in his films, parents wrote angry letters. They said that he was setting a bad example for their children. Walt solved this problem by making up new cartoon characters. They could do all the things that Mickey Mouse couldn't do.

33   Tall, skinny Goofy was so dumb that he always got into trouble. Greedy Pluto kept trying to steal other dogs' bones. Donald Duck was always getting angry. The duck, with his funny, quacking voice, became as famous as Mickey Mouse.

Writing Details

3. Tell what Mickey Mouse looked like and how his voice sounded. (Use complete sentences in your answer.)

4. Write the year in which:
   a. Walt and his wife went on a business trip to New York City (*Hint:* You'll have to figure out this date.)
   b. sound was first used in a movie
   c. sound was first used in a Disney cartoon

Part III

34   **Walt kept on trying** new ideas. He was always ready to look for ways to improve his films. As the first animated cartoon in color, the Disney film *Flowers and Trees* (1932) was a huge success and also made a great deal of money. It even won Walt his first Academy Award for the best cartoon short subject of the year.

35   Walt knew exactly what he wanted. His animated cartoons had to be the very best that could be made. In his studio, he trained his artists carefully. They studied the way a duck walks, the way a bird flies, the way a cat laps up milk. Color artists learned to mix just the right shades for a rose, a snowflake, or a sunset. Actors and musicians spent many hours working on the voices and the tunes to go with the pictures. Walt was willing to spend money, to take risks, and to train his artists for years.

36   By 1934, Walt was ready for something new—something big. Nobody had ever made a full-length animated cartoon. Why not make that another "first" for the Disney studio?

37   The new movie was to be *Snow White and the Seven Dwarfs*. It was to play on the screen for about an hour and a half. Walt figured it might even cost a quarter of a million dollars and take a year and a half to make. By the time the movie was done, it had cost almost two million dollars and taken three years. But it was worth it!

38   Since *Snow White and the Seven Dwarfs* first came out in 1937, it has been shown all over the world. The movie has earned more than 30 million dollars. More important, however, it marked a new direction for Walt Disney. From then on, he made many more full-length animated cartoons, such as *Fantasia*, *Pinocchio*, and *Dumbo*.

39   When Walt first began making films, he had mixed live-action characters and animated cartoons. In later years, he continued to do this. None of the movies of this kind was as successful as *Mary Poppins* (1964).

40   In *Mary Poppins*, everything flows perfectly together. The live actors, the cartoon characters, the many lovely songs and lively dances delighted audiences all over the world. The film earned over 45 million dollars and won several Academy Awards.

Finding the Main Idea

5. Which of the following is the main idea of paragraph 34?
 (*a*) Walt was trying new ideas in films.
 (*b*) He was making a great deal of money.
 (*c*) He won an Academy Award.
 (*d*) none of the above

6. The main idea of paragraphs 36 and 37, which deal with *Snow White and the Seven Dwarfs*, is:
 (*a*) the film's great success
 (*b*) the film's long running time on screen
 (*c*) the story of the making of the film
 (*d*) the secret story behind the making of the film

Part IV

41 **The Disneys had** two daughters—Diane Marie and Sharon Mae. When his daughters were young, Walt had dreamed of building an amusement park just for them. But he could never think small. As the years passed, his idea for an amusement park grew and grew.

42 On July 18, 1955, Walt's dream became reality. In Anaheim, California, he opened the huge amusement park called Disneyland. Visiting Disneyland is like actually being in scenes from Walt Disney's cartoons and movies.

43 "Disneyland will never be finished," Walt said. "It's something we can keep developing and adding to. A motion picture is different. Once it's wrapped up and sent out for processing, we're through with it. If there are things that could be improved, we can't do anything about them any more. I've always wanted to work on something alive, something that keeps growing. We've got that in Disneyland. Even the trees will grow and be more beautiful each year."

Walt Disney World celebrates Mickey Mouse's 60th birthday.

44   Walt enjoyed planning and building Disneyland. He decided to make another, even larger amusement park. This bold plan became Walt Disney World, near Orlando, Florida.

45   While he was working on Disneyland, Walt decided to have his own television program. In the fall of 1954, he began a series of weekly one-hour television shows. They combined Disney cartoons, nature films, and live-action films with advertisements for Disneyland. The host on these shows was Walt himself.

46   In later years, a daily children's show was added—the Mickey Mouse Club. The talented young Mouseketeers on this program were very popular with young children.

47   Walt never stopped planning new projects. He wanted to build a large outdoor resort, or vacation place, in northern California. He also dreamed of a school for artists to be known as Cal Arts.

48   When Walt was 65, his busy life came to an end. A heavy cigarette smoker for many years, he developed lung cancer. He died on December 15, 1966, in Burbank, California. The hospital in which he died was just across the street from the Disney studio.

49   After the death of Walt Disney, Eric Sevareid, a CBS newscaster, said this:

50   It would take more time than anybody has around the daily news shops to think of the right thing to say about Walt Disney.

51   He was an original; not just an American original, but an original, period. He was a happy accident; one of the happiest this century has experienced; and judging by the way it's been behaving in spite of all Disney tried to tell it about laughter, love, children, puppies, and sunrises, the century hardly deserved him.

52   But what Walt Disney seemed to know was that while there is very lit-

tle grown-up in a child, there is a lot of child in every grown-up. To a child this weary world is brand-new, gift wrapped; Disney tried to keep it that way for adults.

Working with Words

7. Use the following list of related words to supply the missing words below.

> animated (paragraph 5)
> animation
> animator

a. An _____ draws many slightly different pictures of the same cartoon figure.

b. To produce the effect of _____ , all the pictures are photographed with movie film.

c. When the film is shown on a screen, the result is an _____ cartoon.

8. The word *frustrated* (paragraph 10) most nearly means:
(*a*) sick (*b*) discouraged (*c*) delighted (*d*) satisfied

9. An *award* (paragraph 34) is a kind of:
(*a*) cartoon (*b*) subject (*c*) speech (*d*) prize

10. A *weary* (paragraph 52) person would probably prefer to:
(*a*) dance (*b*) wear jewelry (*c*) rest (*d*) study hard

EXERCISES

Putting Events in Sequence

A. Write the letters of each set of events in the order in which the events happened in Walt Disney's life. For example, would you answer #1 by writing *a-b* or *b-a?* If you need help, look back at the story.

1. *a.* Walt sets up his own animated cartoon company, Laugh-O-Gram Films.
   b. He moves to Hollywood, California.

2. *a.* Walt makes his first drawings of Mickey Mouse.
   b. He marries Lillian Bounds.

3. *a.* Walt creates Goofy, Pluto, Donald Duck, and other new cartoon characters.
   b. Mickey Mouse becomes a superstar.

4. *a.* The Disney studio produces the first animated cartoons with sound and color.
   b. *Snow White and the Seven Dwarfs*, the first full-length animated cartoon, appears.

5. *a.* The Disneys have two daughters.
   b. Disneyland and Walt Disney World are opened to the public.

Making Inferences

B. Use what you have read about Walt Disney to infer, or figure out, the correct choice.

1. If Walt heard of a new way to make animated cartoons, he would probably:
   (*a*) ignore it   (*b*) claim it was his   (*c*) try it   (*d*) reject it

2. You can infer that sound was first added to a movie by:
   (*a*) Walt Disney   (*b*) Roy Disney
   (*c*) Laugh-O-Gram Films   (*d*) someone else

3. Which of the following is an inference?
   (*a*) Walt combined real people in live action with animated cartoons early in his career.
   (*b*) When Walt took risks, he generally was successful and made money.
   (*c*) Mickey Mouse's voice was always that of Walt Disney.
   (*d*) *Snow White and the Seven Dwarfs* first came out in 1937.

4. The word that best describes Walt is:
   (*a*) perfectionist   (*b*) lazy   (*c*) scholar   (*d*) foolish

Understanding Cause and Effect

C. Write the letter of the best choice.

1. Walt decided to move to California because:
   (*a*) he liked the climate
   (*b*) his wife-to-be lived there
   (*c*) he hoped to be more successful there
   (*d*) his brother Roy urged him to go there

2. The single most important cause of Walt's early success was:
   (*a*) Donald Duck   (*b*) *Mary Poppins*
   (*c*) Disneyland   (*d*) Mickey Mouse

3. As a result of the successful production of *Snow White and the Seven Dwarfs*, the Disney studio:
   (*a*) created a new cartoon character
   (*b*) started making nature films
   (*c*) made more full-length cartoons
   (*d*) set up a weekly television program

4. Walt was especially excited about Disneyland because it would:
   (*a*) make a lot of money
   (*b*) change and grow
   (*c*) advertise his cartoons
   (*d*) please his two daughters

Separating Fact from Opinion

D. Tell which is a *fact* and which is an *opinion*.

1. Early cartoons were in black and white.

2. Color cartoons are better than black-and-white ones.

3. *Mary Poppins* is a perfect work of art.

4. An animated cartoon should not be judged by the same standards used to judge a live-action film.

Choosing the Best Title

E.   Write the number of the best title for the story of Walt Disney.

1. Early Animated Cartoons

2. Walt Disney's Life and Career

3. How Mickey Mouse Was Born

4. Movies and Theme Parks

Speaking, Listening, and Writing

F.   **Dictation:** With your book closed and a sheet of paper and a pen or pencil for taking notes, listen while your teacher reads aloud a brief passage from the story of Walt Disney. Then answer the questions your teacher asks.

(*Note:* The questions appear in a separate Answer Key.)

G.   Write a paragraph or more about one of the following topics.

1. What are some of the new things that Walt Disney tried in his films?

2. Walt was not only a filmmaker. Tell about some other things he did.

3. Write a letter to a friend telling him or her what your favorite Walt Disney movie is and why.

How do you start a school with a dollar and a half and a dream?

10. *Mary McLeod Bethune*

Part I

1   **Mary McLeod was born** in South Carolina in 1875. The Civil War had ended just 10 years before, and enslaved people had been set free. It was a time of new hope for her family and for black people in America.

2   On a shelf in her house stood the one book the McLeods owned—their beloved Bible. Yet not one of the 20 members of her large family was able to read it. In those times, very few black people in the South could read or write. Under slavery, it had been against the law.

3   There seemed little hope that Mary could go to school. There were no schools for black children where she lived. Also, the family was poor. With so many mouths to feed, everyone had to help with the work. Along with her brothers and sisters, Mary picked cotton on the family's five acres.

4   One morning, a stranger appeared at the farm. "I'm Miss Emma Wilson," the black woman said.

5   Mary's mouth opened with astonishment. She had never heard black people called by anything but their first names. *Miss* Wilson. It sounded wonderful. Some day, Mary decided, people—even white people—would call *her* Miss McLeod.

6   Miss Wilson explained that the Presbyterian Mission Board was starting a school for black children. She would be the teacher at the school in the town of Mayesville, five miles from the farm. Could some of the McLeod children go?

7   Mr. and Mrs. McLeod knew that the children were needed to help at home. But perhaps they could spare one child. They looked at Mary. Her eyes were glowing. Yes, she was the one to go to school. Maybe she would even learn to read the Bible to the whole family. So it was decided.

8   Mary loved the little school in Mayesville. She was a good student, and Miss Wilson was proud of her. On graduation day, the whole McLeod family and their friends and neighbors crowded into the school. The day Mary finished all her school courses was a great moment in the lives of them all.

9   After that, Mary had to go back to work on the farm. Her father and mother needed her more than ever. Besides, there was no other school nearby. It looked as if Mary's education had come to an end.

Finding Details

1. In which paragraph do you learn:
   a. who would be Mary's teacher
   b. what Mary did on her family's farm
   c. where the new school would be
   d. when Mary was born

2. Give the numbers of the two paragraphs that tell where Mary lived and went to school as a child.

Part II

10   **Once again,** Miss Emma Wilson appeared at the farm. "Great news!" the teacher cried. "Mary can go on with her schooling."

11   "But where will the money come from?" Mrs. McLeod asked.

12   "Someone has given money to help a young black person go to school," Miss Wilson said.

13   "Who is this rich man?" asked Mrs. McLeod.

14   Miss Wilson smiled. "It's not a rich man," she said. "It's a poor Quaker woman named Miss Mary Crissman. She lives in Denver, Colorado, and she's a dressmaker. For years, she's been saving 10 cents out of every dollar she earned to help a black child through school."

15   With Miss Crissman's help, Mary studied for seven years at the Scotia Seminary, a school for black girls in North Carolina. Besides learning history, algebra, and Latin, she also learned new things about herself.

16   She discovered that she had a deep and beautiful singing voice. With other students from the college, she began to sing in public. She also learned that she could speak well in public. Both these talents helped her later in her life.

17   After college, Mary became a schoolteacher in the South. While teaching in South Carolina, she met Albertus Bethune, also a schoolteacher. They married and moved to Florida, where they both taught school for several years. Although Albertus was content in his work, Mary was not.

18   "Someday," she told herself, "I will have a school of my own. It will be for black girls who need the chance to learn, as I once did."

19   To start a school, Mary needed two things—children to teach and money for the school. In 1904, she began to hear exciting things about the city of Daytona Beach. A man named Henry Flagler was putting up a big hotel on the east coast of Florida at Daytona Beach.

He was also building a railroad to bring people from the North down to his hotel. From all over the South, black families were moving to Daytona Beach to work on the railroad. There would be more jobs for them at Mr. Flagler's hotel.

20 "Daytona Beach sounds like the right place for my school," Mary said to her husband. "I could teach the children there. And who knows? Some of those people at the hotel might even help me out with money for my school."

21 Albertus shook his head. It all sounded like a foolish dream to him. Besides, he wanted to stay where he was. So Mary moved to Daytona Beach without him. In her pocket, she had just one dollar and 50 cents.

22 In Daytona Beach, she visited black families and made friends who helped her. She even found five little girls to be her first students. She also found a house in which to start her school. But what a house!

23 It was a dirty old building. Most of the windows were broken, and the roof leaked. Beyond the building was a huge dump. Since the house did have five large rooms, however, she decided it would do.

24 The owner of the building agreed to rent it to her for 11 dollars a month. Of course, Mary didn't have 11 dollars. She talked the owner into taking her one dollar and 50 cents as part payment. She had made up her mind that she would raise the rest of the money—somehow.

Writing Details

1. Write the missing name in each of the following sentences. If you need help, look back to Part II of the story.
   a. _____ brought the good news that Mary could continue her education.
   b. _____ made it possible for Mary to go on with her education.
   c. After college, Mary and _____ were married.
   d. _____ built a hotel and a railroad in Daytona Beach, Florida.

2. There are several details about money in Part II. Using complete sentences, write:
   a. what percent of her income Miss Mary Crissman saved each year to help educate a black child (*Hint:* You'll have to figure out this answer.)
   b. who Mary McLeod Bethune hoped would contribute money for her new school
   c. how much money Mary had when she moved to Daytona Beach, Florida
   d. how much more money Mary needed to pay the rent for her new school (*Hint:* You'll have to figure out this answer, too.)

Part III

25   **With her five little girls,** Mary searched through the streets of Daytona Beach and even in the dump for school supplies. They found old wooden boxes for seats and desks. They took broken chairs and cracked dishes. When she went to the store, she asked the storekeeper for a separate piece of wrapping paper for each item. Her students wrote their lessons on the wrapping paper. Bit by bit, Mary created her school, putting it together with hard work and anything she could find.

26   Mary taught her girls to sing in a group. She took them to the Flagler Hotel, where they sang for the guests. When she spoke of her plans to the guests, she had a way of making her dreams sound real. More and more people began to give money to help build her school.

27   At last, on October 4, 1904, Mary opened her new school. Her students were the five little girls. Whenever they could, the families of the girls paid her 50 cents a week. Over the door of her school, Mary had written: "Enter to Learn. Depart to Serve." These were not empty words. She made sure that when her students left her school, they used what they had learned to help others.

28   Mary knew how important education was for her people. She also knew how important it was for them to use their right to vote. At election time, she urged black Americans to vote.

29   In those days, some white people did not want black children to have an education. They also didn't want black men and women to vote. They tried to stop them by forming the Ku Klux Klan. Klan members usually rode at night. Dressed in white sheets and carrying guns and whips, they used threats and force to keep black people "in their place."

30   Shortly before a local election, Mary was warned that the Klan was coming. At night, she turned on all the lights in the school building, and she sent the younger girls to bed. Outside the front door of her school, she stood alone, waiting.

31   Hours passed, and still she waited. At last, she heard the sound of horses coming. She saw the flicker of torches moving toward her. Under the unsteady, moving lights, 80 white-robed figures rode into the schoolyard.

32   "We hear you're telling colored people to vote," one of the masked men said. He was holding a large can of kerosene. "You keep on like that, and we'll burn your school down."

33   The masked man slowly climbed down from his horse. He set the can of kerosene on the ground.

34   Mary stood up straight and tall. "You can burn my school down," she said. "But if you do, I'll just build it up again. And again and again!"

35   Just then, the sound of singing rang out from the lighted windows of the school. The music grew louder and seemed to fill the night. It was the older girls lifting their voices in a hymn.

36   Forgetting all about the can of kerosene, the masked man leaped back onto his horse. The white-robed Klansmen turned and rode away into the night. Mary breathed a deep sigh of relief and called the school janitor.

37   "Put that can of kerosene away," she said calmly. "We can find a good use for it."

Finding the Main Idea

5. The main idea of paragraph 25 is best expressed by which sentence?
   (*a*) first   (*b*) second   (*c*) fourth   (*d*) last

6. The main idea of paragraph 26 is:
   (*a*) People were staying at the Flagler Hotel.
   (*b*) Mary taught her girls to sing.
   (*c*) She raised funds for the school.
   (*d*) She made friends with the guests.

Part IV

38   **As her school grew larger,** Mary managed to find a good use for everything. For 20 years, she used all her talents and all her energy to keep her school going and growing. But what if she became ill? Who would raise the money to pay all the bills? There were now six boys in her school. She felt that there should be more boys. Where would they come from?

39   The answers to these questions lay in the Cookman Institute of Jacksonville, Florida. This school for black boys was run by the Methodist Church. In 1923, Mary's school joined the Cookman Institute, with Mary as president. The new name of the school was the Bethune-Cookman College. The Methodist Church agreed to take over the problems of raising money.

40   Now Mary had more time to serve her people and her country in new ways. She could give her great energy, wisdom, and love to all of America.

41   She became a good friend of Eleanor Roosevelt, the wife of President Franklin Delano Roosevelt. The two women often worked together, trying to help black people and white people get along better. Mary also helped set up the National Council of Negro Women, serving as its president for many years. In addition, she worked for more than 50 other organizations. Four presidents of the United States—Coolidge, Hoover, Roosevelt, and Truman—asked her for advice and help.

42   Over the years, Mary was honored for her great service to America. Eleven colleges and universities awarded her honorary degrees. Several nations gave her medals. All over the world, she was loved and respected.

43   Before her death in 1955, Mary McLeod Bethune wrote a will. Most people write wills in which they tell who will get the things they own when they die. In Mary's will, she said that she had never owned many things, but that she was very rich in experiences. She wanted to leave the following "things" to black people everywhere:

I leave you love.
I leave you hope.
I leave you a thirst for education.
I leave you faith.
I leave you racial dignity.
I leave you a desire to live harmoniously with your fellow men.
I leave you finally a responsibility to our young people.

Working with Words

7. *Astonishment* (paragraph 5) most nearly means:
   (*a*) disappointment   (*b*) anger   (*c*) sorrow   (*d*) surprise

8. A person who is *content* (paragraph 17) would NOT want to:
  (*a*) change   (*b*) understand
  (*c*) remain the same   (*d*) believe the facts

9. To *depart* (paragraph 27) is most nearly the OPPOSITE of:
  (*a*) to put together   (*b*) to arrive
  (*c*) to please   (*d*) to annoy

10. *Organizations* (paragraph 41) are most likely to have:
  (*a*) Presidents of the United States
  (*b*) gold medals and honorary degrees
  (*c*) people with the same interests and goals
  (*d*) things included in a will

EXERCISES

Putting Events in Sequence

A. Write the letters of each set of events in the order in which the events happened in Mary McLeod Bethune's life. For example, would you answer #1 by writing *a-b* or *b-a*? If you need help, look back at the story.

1. *a.* Mary goes to school.
  b. The Civil War ends.

2. *a.* She moves to Florida.
  b. She becomes a schoolteacher.

3. *a.* Henry Flagler begins to build a big hotel in Daytona Beach, Florida.
  b. Mary goes to Daytona Beach.

4. *a.* The Ku Klux Klan visits her school at night.
  b. She urges blacks in Daytona Beach to vote.

5. *a.* She becomes president of Bethune-Cookman College.
  b. She works with Eleanor Roosevelt.

Making Inferences

   B.   Use what you have read about Mary McLeod Bethune to infer, or figure out, the correct choice.

1. Which of the following is an inference?
   (*a*) The McLeod's owned only one book—a Bible.
   (*b*) No one in the family could read it.
   (*c*) Slaves had not been allowed to read.
   (*d*) Mary's parents never read the newspapers.

2. Which of the following is a direct statement, NOT an infer-ence?
   (*a*) Mary must have been an intelligent child.
   (*b*) Miss Mary Crissman was a Quaker.
   (*c*) Albertus Bethune didn't like to take risks.
   (*d*) Henry Flagler was willing to take risks.

3. Mary believed that the chief purpose of learning should be:
   (*a*) for its own sake
   (*b*) to make money
   (*c*) to help others
   (*d*) to build one's self-confidence

4. The phrase "in their place" (paragraph 29) is in quotation marks because:
   (*a*) Mary might have said it
   (*b*) the school janitor might have said it
   (*c*) a member of the Klan might have said it
   (*d*) one of Mary's students might have said it

Understanding Cause and Effect

   C.   Write the letter of the correct choice.

1. An important cause of Mary's desire to help others was the help she received from:
   (*a*) her husband   (*b*) a poor Quaker woman
   (*c*) Henry Flagler   (*d*) Eleanor Roosevelt

2. One effect of Henry Flagler's development of the east coast of Florida was:
   (*a*) voting rights for black people
   (*b*) better relations between black people and white people
   (*c*) an increase in Ku Klux Klan membership
   (*d*) jobs for black people

3. By riding at night to Mary's school, the Ku Klux Klan hoped to:
   (*a*) discourage black people from getting an education
   (*b*) keep black people from voting
   (*c*) frighten Mary
   (*d*) all of the above

4. Mary approved of the union of her school with the Cookman Institute because:
   (*a*) both black children and white children could attend the new school
   (*b*) it freed her to do other important things
   (*c*) Eleanor Roosevelt would teach at the new school
   (*d*) Mary could earn more money

Separating Fact from Opinion

   D. Tell which is a *fact* and which is an *opinion*.

1. Mary was never a wealthy woman.

2. She deserved to have more money than she did.

3. The Klan threatened to burn down Mary's school.

4. Few people would have the courage to stand up to the Klan as Mary did.

Choosing the Best Title

   E. Write the number of the best title for the story of Mary McLeod Bethune.

1. Facing the Ku Klux Klan

2. Teacher of Her People

3. Advisor to Presidents

4. Education for All Americans

Speaking, Listening, and Writing

F.   Be prepared to talk about one of the following. (You may wish to make up a name for the real person you choose to tell about.)

1. Tell about someone you know who could not go to school. What kept this person from getting an education?

2. Tell about someone you know who had a hard time going to school but did anyway. What happened to this person?

G.   Write a paragraph or more about one of the following topics.

1. What are some of the ways in which Mary raised money for her school?

2. Mary was a brave woman. In a brief article for your school newspaper, mention some facts of her life that show how brave she was.

3. How did other people help Mary along in her life?

A Mexican-American farm worker fights to win a decent life for other farm workers.

11. Cesar Chavez

Part I

1   **Have you ever heard** of the United Farm Workers (UFW)? Of *la causa*? Or of the man behind these things— Cesar Chavez? A governor of California has written, "Cesar Chavez is one of the great men of California today." Senator Robert Kennedy called him "one of the heroic figures of our times."

2   Cesar was born in Arizona in 1927 into a Mexican-American, or *Chicano*, family. He had four brothers and sisters. As a child, he lived on his family's small farm near Yuma, Arizona.

3   In the 1930s, hard times came. These were the years of the Great Depression. The Chavez family lost their farm because they could not pay their taxes. When Cesar was 10, the family moved to California, hoping to find work there.

4   The Chavez family became migrant farm workers. They moved from farm to farm, wherever there were fruits and vegetables to pick. They picked these crops for the farm owners, or growers, the white Americans whom the Chicanos call *Anglos*.

5   During these years, Cesar learned how hard life was for his people. With his family, he picked fruits and vegetables from 1937 to 1942 on the huge farms in the great Central Valley of California. However long or hard they

125

Migrant farm workers in California.

worked, they never had enough money. They often had little to eat. The whole family had to keep moving to find work.

6   By the time he was 15 years old, Cesar had changed schools 36 times. No wonder he was still in the eighth grade! In school, he was treated like a child; but in the fields, he worked like a man.

7   While Cesar was still a teenager, he decided he was old enough to go to work on his own. For three years, he traveled from farm to farm alone, picking fruits and vegetables. Although he was a quiet, shy young man, he made friends among the Mexican-American and Filipino migrant workers. (Many migrant farm workers in California are Filipinos, from islands called the Philippines, far across the Pacific Ocean.)

8   In the town of Delano, Cesar began to go out with a young woman named Helen Fabela. When he was 19 years old, he felt ready to start a family of his own. Helen and he were married in the big Catholic church of Delano. All the young couple could look forward to was

the hard life of the migrant worker. During the next four years, they had three children. Later there would be eight children in the Chavez family.

9   Cesar bought an old station wagon in which the whole family drove together looking for work. When there was no work in the fields, they lived in a very poor section of San Jose called *Sal Si Puedes*. In English, this means "Get out if you can." It was the perfect name for such a place. Few Chicanos could get out of the life of hard work, poor pay, and no hope.

10   One day in 1952, a man named Fred Ross came looking for Cesar Chavez. Fred worked for the Community Service Organization, or CSO. The CSO helped poor people learn how to help themselves. It was very active among the migrant farm workers.

11   Fred was a tall, thin white man—an Anglo. At first, Cesar didn't trust him. He had already had enough trouble from Anglos. As the two men talked, however, Cesar began to like this stranger. But Fred had no easy answers.

12   "You have to work out the answers for yourself," he said. "The CSO can only try to help you do this."

13   "But how?" Cesar asked.

14   "It takes time and hard work. Your people must learn to be strong. They can find a way to make their lives better."

15   "*Sal si puedes*," Cesar thought. "Maybe the CSO can help us."

Finding Details

1. Give the number of the paragraph that tells:
   a. where the Chavez family moved after they lost their farm
   b. how often Cesar changed schools
   c. what *Sal Si Puedes* means
   d. who worked for the CSO

2. You read about Cesar's wife and children in paragraphs:
(*a*) 2 and 3   (*b*) 5 and 6   (*c*) 8 and 9   (*d*) 10 and 11

Part II

16   **Cesar Chavez** joined the CSO. At first, he worked in the evenings without pay and picked crops during the day. After a while, he became a paid worker for the CSO. In 1958, he became its general director in California.

17   He learned a great deal from Fred Ross. The older man told him about the National Labor Relations Act of 1935. This law gave factory workers all over the nation the right to form unions. However, the law did not cover farm workers. They didn't have the right to form unions.

18   "How can farm workers make a fair living?" Cesar said at a meeting of the CSO. "They must have a union."

19   "It's been tried many times before," the CSO people told him. "The growers are just too strong. They have the laws and the police on their side. If the farm workers try to form a union, the growers will crush them."

20   "I believe it can be done," Cesar said. "It *must* be done!"

21   In 1962, Cesar left the CSO. From Los Angeles, he went back to Delano. It was hard to give up a good, steady job, but he felt he had more important work to do.

22   "It's going to be tough," he said to his wife. "We have only $1200 in savings and our old station wagon. They'll both have to last a long time."

23   "We'll manage," Helen assured him. "We'll all work together."

24   Making a living was hard enough, but building a union was even harder. Luckily, Cesar and Helen were

not alone. Cesar's younger brother Richard and his cousin Manuel helped. A number of good friends also joined them there. They were all like one big family.

25   They called their union the National Farm Workers Association. To the growers, *union* was a dirty word. Also, the law did not give farm workers the right to form unions. But who could object to an *Association*? The Association even had its own flag. Drawn by Cousin Manuel, it showed a black eagle with wide-open wings.

26   Cesar knew how the Association must work. It had to help the people both in their work and in their personal lives. It had to reach out and touch their hearts. In all these ways and more, the Association had to serve the migrant farm workers' cause. In Spanish, they called it *la causa*.

27   They established a credit union, which is a kind of people's bank. In times of great need, poor farm workers could borrow money from it. People also came to Cesar for help or advice. When they were in trouble, they often turned to him.

28   By the end of 1964, the Association had a thousand members. Each member paid dues of $3.50 a month. Since migrant farm workers needed every penny, this was no small sum.

29   Building the Association was slow work. In 1965, Cesar did not think that they were ready for a test of strength against the growers. As it turned out, he had no choice.

Writing Details

3. Write the missing details in each of the following.
   a. The _____ was the law that gave factory workers the right to form unions.
   b. Cesar gave up his job with the CSO in order to _____.
   c. To avoid trouble, the farm workers' union was called a(an) _____.

4. Using complete sentences, tell:
   a. why a union for farm workers had never been formed before
   b. who helped Cesar build the National Farm Workers Association
   c. in what town the Association was founded (first formed)

Part III

30   **A small union** of Filipino farm workers had gone out on strike for better pay. They were on strike against the growers of grapes used to make wine. Their leader, Larry Itliong, asked Cesar Chavez and the National Farm Workers Association to join them. The members of the Association voted to join the strike. And so, in September 1965, the big strike—*la huelga*—began.

31   The farm workers soon found that their strike posed special problems. A strike by workers in a factory or a store is relatively simple. The union members don't go to work. Groups or lines of striking workers, called pickets, march up and down in front of the doors of the building. A strike by farm workers is not so simple. Unlike a factory or a store, a farm doesn't have a front door or a back door. How do you form a picket line around miles and miles of farmland?

32   There were other problems. The growers were banded together in the strong American Farm Bureau Federation. They had millions of dollars. The National Farm Workers Association had only 82 dollars.

33   Cesar and his friends asked for help and money. People from all over the country gave what they could. College students and religious leaders joined the picket lines. Unions and other groups sent food, clothing, and money for the strikers and their families.

34   When the union members went out on strike, the growers brought in farm workers from Mexico as strikebreakers to take their place. As the strike dragged on, the growers seemed to be winning. The work was being done by the strikebreakers. The grapes were being picked.

35   "We can't stop the growers from bringing in strikebreakers to pick the grapes," Cesar thought. "But we can tell people all over America not to buy their wine."

36   He sent members of the Association to the big cities of America. They visited stores where California wines were sold. They urged people to boycott (not to buy) these wines.

37   The whole nation began to take notice of the farm workers' strike in California. In March 1966, a group of United States senators went to California to look into the problems of the migrant farm workers. In that same month, Cesar thought of something else to win national support for *la causa*. He had heard of the success of the peaceful freedom marches of Martin Luther King, Jr., in the South. Why not do the same thing in California?

38   On March 18, 1966, Cesar led about 200 farm workers on a march. They walked 300 miles from Delano to Sacramento, the capital city of California. They marched there to ask the governor for a state law giving farm workers the right to form unions. On April 10, Easter Sunday, a crowd of about 10 thousand people gathered in Sacramento to greet the tired marchers. They sang "We Shall Overcome" in Spanish—"*Nosotros Venceremos.*"

39   One after another, the big growers of wine grapes began to sign contracts with the unions. They agreed to pay better wages and to desist from spraying the fields with bug and weed poisons that could hurt the farm workers. In general, the contracts gave the union members better working conditions.

40   Most important, the growers agreed to use union hiring halls. When a grower needed farm workers, he had to get them from the union. Workers would no longer be cheated or treated badly. Their union would take care of them.

Finding the Main Idea

5. The main idea of paragraphs 31 and 32 is:
   (*a*) There are many differences between strikes in a factory and on a farm.
   (*b*) The growers have power and wealth.
   (*c*) Striking factory workers face all kinds of problems.
   (*d*) The striking farm workers had to face many problems.

6. The main idea of paragraph 34 concerns:
   (*a*) striking farm workers   (*b*) strikebreakers   (*c*) growers
   (*d*) grapes

Part IV

41   **Cesar knew** that the fight with the growers had just begun, that it would be a long, hard struggle. *La causa* would need all the money, help, and friends it could find. For this reason, the National Farm Workers Association and Larry Itliong's union joined forces. The name of the new union was the United Farm Workers, but people simply called it the UFW. Cesar became the director of the UFW, and Larry became the assistant director.

42   The growers of wine grapes were signing contracts with the UFW. But the growers of grapes for eating— table grapes—would not even talk to the union.

Cesar Chavez is at the left.

43   Cesar Chavez and his UFW went on strike again. They asked people not to buy any table grapes from California. The union sent a group of its own actors, singers, and musicians, the *Teatro Campesino*, to all the big cities. With song, dance, and humor, it told people about *la causa*.

44   When violence flared up between angry growers and strikers, Cesar fasted. For 25 days, he ate no food. He wanted nobody killed or even hurt. By fasting, Cesar wanted to turn his people away from violence. He believed that even a single human life was worth more than the union.

45   "If we become violent with others," he said, "then we will become violent among ourselves. Social justice for the dignity of man cannot be won at the price of human life."

46   For two more years, the struggle between the UFW and the table grape growers went on. But the strike and the boycott finally forced the growers to give in. In 1970, about 85 percent of the table-grape growers signed union contracts.

47   Not all these contracts, however, were made with the UFW. Some of the growers signed contracts with another union, the Teamsters' Union. That union helped the growers to keep the old system the way it was. They even agreed to do away with union hiring halls. This old system put the farm workers right back in the power of the growers.

48   Despite these difficulties, Cesar and the UFW kept their faith and persisted in their fight for the migrant farm workers. As a result, they won two important victories.

49   In 1975, a friend of the farm workers was elected governor of California. Governor Edmund G. Brown, Jr., put through the first state law ever to give farm workers the right to form unions. This law was the California Agricultural Labor Relations Act. In 1977, the United Farm Workers and the Teamsters' Union made peace. They worked out a plan that would be fair to both sides. The UFW would organize only farm workers who worked in the fields, while the Teamsters' Union would organize the other workers.

50   In the 1980s, Cesar Chavez turned his attention to the problem of pesticides. These are poisons sprayed on fruits and vegetables to kill insects. For the farm workers who must handle the fruits and vegetables in the fields, some of these pesticides cause serious illness. Once again, the UFW asked people to boycott table grapes

from California. Once again, Cesar fasted to call attention to *la causa*.

51   Against constant difficulties and setbacks, the struggle to win a better life for farm workers and their families goes on. Farm workers in California have learned to work together and to be strong. Migrant farm workers all over America are better off today because of Cesar Chavez and his belief in *la causa*.

Working with Words

7. Use the following list of related words to write the missing words below.

   migrant (paragraph 4)
   migrate
   migration
   immigrant

   a. After the Chavez family lost their farm in Arizona, they decided to _____ to California.

   b. A person who comes to live in a new country is a(an) _____.

   c. The movement of people or animals from one place to live in another is called _____.

   d. A(An) _____ worker moves about in search of work.

8. A word that is most nearly the OPPOSITE of *national* (paragraph 17) is:
   (*a*) illegal   (*b*) local   (*c*) temporary   (*d*) native

9. If the growers agreed to *desist* (paragraph 39) from spraying poisons, they must have:
   (*a*) stopped   (*b*) started   (*c*) continued   (*d*) never begun

10. *Violence* (paragraph 44) is often the result of:
   (*a*) sorrow   (*b*) anger   (*c*) fasting   (*d*) discussion

EXERCISES

Putting Events in Sequence

A. Write the letters of each set of events in the order in which the events happened in Cesar Chavez's life. For example, would you answer #1 by writing *a-b* or *b-a*? If you need help, look back at the story.

1. *a.* The Chavez family moves to California.
   b. They lose their farm in Arizona.

2. *a.* Cesar meets Fred Ross.
   b. Cesar works for the Community Service Organization.

3. *a.* The National Farm Workers Association starts a boycott of California wines.
   b. The association goes on strike against the growers of wine grapes in California.

4. *a.* Cesar calls a strike against the table grape growers of California.
   b. The United Farm Workers (UFW) is formed.

5. *a.* The growers begin to sign contracts with the Teamsters' Union.
   b. The California Labor Relations Act becomes law.

Making Inferences

B. Use what you have read about Cesar Chavez to infer, or figure out, the correct choice.

1. Cesar changed school 36 times because:
   (*a*) he disliked school
   (*b*) he was treated like a child in school
   (*c*) his native language was Spanish rather than English
   (*d*) his family was constantly moving

2. When Cesar first met Fred Ross, the trouble Cesar had already had from Anglos chiefly involved those who were:
   (*a*) Filipinos   (*b*) farm workers   (*c*) growers   (*d*) Chicanos

3. You can infer that Cesar would NOT approve the use of:
   (*a*) boycotts (*b*) pickets (*c*) marches (*d*) guns

4. In the 1980s, Cesar's concern for farm workers focused on their:
   (*a*) right to work   (*b*) right to strike
   (*c*) health   (*d*) education

Understanding Cause and Effect

    C.   Write the letter of the best choice.

1. A direct effect of Fred Ross's conversations with Cesar was to:
   (*a*) form the first farm workers' union
   (*b*) lead Cesar to join the CSO
   (*c*) inspire Cesar to complete his education
   (*d*) make Cesar move to Delano

2. California grape growers disliked a boycott chiefly because it hurt their:
   (*a*) workers (*b*) competitors (*c*) profits (*d*) grapes

3. Because of violence during a strike, Cesar:
   (*a*) ended the strike
   (*b*) took the growers to court
   (*c*) marched to Sacramento
   (*d*) decided to fast

4. As a result of the election of Edmund G. Brown, Jr., a state law was passed:
   (*a*) banning pesticides
   (*b*) giving farm workers the right to form unions
   (*c*) making peace between the Teamsters' Union and the UFW
   (*d*) prohibiting the use of strikebreakers in labor disputes

Separating Fact from Opinion

    D.   Tell which is a *fact* and which is an *opinion*.

1. Cesar Chavez is one of the great men of California today.

2. A governor of California has written, "Cesar Chavez is one of the great men of California today."

3. Cesar once fasted for 25 days.

4. Before 1977, the Teamsters' Union was a rival of the UFW.

Choosing the Best Title

E. Write the number of the best title for the story of Cesar Chavez.

1. The Man Behind *La Causa*

2. The Teamsters' Union

3. The California Farm System

4. Migrant Farm Workers

Speaking, Listening, and Writing

F. In small groups, at your teacher's direction, discuss one of the following topics.

1. Mexican-Americans are only one minority group in the United States. Name some others. What problems do you think these minority groups share.

2. Are there any groups of migrant farm workers in your state? If so, who are they? If not, can you explain why there are none?

G. Write a paragraph or more about one of the following topics.

1. Tell about some of the things Cesar did to persuade the grape growers to sign contracts with his union.

2. Do you think Cesar was wise not to use force or violence against the growers? Write a letter to Cesar explaining your point of view.

3. In what way was Cesar "one of the heroic figures of our time?" How was he a hero?

Even the world's fastest human has to earn a living.

12. Jesse Owens

Part I

1   **Jesse Owens was** one of America's most famous track stars. He could run faster and jump farther than any other human being. The newspapers called him "the world's fastest human."

2   But Jesse was more than a great athlete. He was a man who believed in this country. As he once said, "In America, anyone can still become somebody."

3   If anyone knew that, it was Jesse. His family was very poor, and he was sickly as a young child. At first, he had a hard time just staying alive.

4   Born in 1913, Jesse lived with his six brothers and sisters on a farm in Alabama. For the Owens family, home was a broken-down wooden shack. The roof leaked. In the summer, the shack was as hot as an oven. In the winter, the wind blew right through the thin walls.

5   Every winter, all during the cold weather, Jesse was sick. His parents called his sickness the "devil's cold." One year, the "devil's cold" and the winter winds almost killed little Jesse. Although his mother nursed him back to health, she was afraid that he would not live through another winter in that paper-thin shack.

6   Hoping that life would be easier for all of them up North, Jesse's father moved his family to Cleveland, Ohio. For Jesse, who was then eight years old, the move marked the beginning of a new life.

7   Jesse was in the fourth grade in elementary school. The athletic coach for both the elementary school and high school was a white man named Charles Riley. One day, he stopped to talk to Jesse.

8   "I've been watching you," he said with a friendly smile. "How about coming out for my track team? It would help build up your skinny legs."

9   Every morning, Mr. Riley met Jesse at the athletic field. The coach carried a big watch on the end of a piece of rope. He taught Jesse how to run like a real racer.

10   Mr. Riley was more than a coach. He was like a second father to Jesse. When he saw that the boy was not

getting enough to eat, he brought him food cooked by his wife. In his own quiet way, Mr. Riley taught Jesse much more than how to run. Many years later, Jesse said, "He trained me to become a man as well as an athlete."

11   By the time Jesse reached high school, all the training had changed him. His legs had filled out, and his whole body had grown stronger.

12   One day, Jesse ran so fast that Mr. Riley couldn't believe what he saw. He checked his watch. Yes, it was 9.4 seconds. He even measured the distance again. It was exactly 100 yards. No doubt about it! Although Jesse Owens was still only a high school student, he had just tied the world record for the 100-yard dash!

Finding Details

1. The number of the paragraph in which you learn where the Owens family moved is:
   (*a*) 4   (*b*) 5   (*c*) 6   (*d*) 7

2. In which group of paragraphs do you find details about:
   a. Jesse as a grown man
   b. Jesse before he was eight years old
   c. Jesse's first athletic coach
   d. Jesse in high school

Part II

13   **While he was still in high school,** Jesse took on new responsibilities. He married Ruth Solomon, a girl he had known since he was 11 years old. Early in their marriage, the young couple had a baby. Around this time, Jesse's father lost his job. Now Jesse had to work hard to help support two families.

14   He also ran harder than ever. His speed set new

track records. The name Jesse Owens was becoming known throughout the sports world.

15   Colleges all over the country wanted him as a student. Each one promised him a lot of money if he would join its track team. But Jesse felt he couldn't take money just for running while his own father was out of work. He turned down all the offers.

16   Once more Charles Riley helped. He talked to people at Ohio State University. They got Jesse three part-time jobs, and they even found a good job for his father. Now Jesse could go to college.

17   At Ohio State, the athletic coach was Larry Snyder. Like Charles Riley, he worked hard with Jesse. Under Coach Snyder's training, Jesse was turning into a great athlete.

18   A big day was coming. On May 25, 1935, the best college track athletes in America were going to compete in Michigan. Jesse would represent Ohio State at this important track meet. A few days before the meet, however, Jesse hurt his back. He was in such great pain that he had to be helped to stand up and sit down. On the day of the track meet, he was still in terrible pain.

19   "I can't let you run today," Coach Snyder said. "You could hurt yourself even worse."

20   "Please, coach," Jesse pleaded. "At least let me try the 100-yard dash. That's a short one. I know I can do it."

21   Jesse had his way. Despite his sore back, he ran the 100 yards in 9.4 seconds. He had tied the world's record again.

22   "I have a good feeling about today," Jesse said to his coach. "I want to try the broad jump, too. My back seems OK."

23   Coach Snyder nodded. If Jesse felt he could go on, he wouldn't stop him.

24   The world record for the broad jump was 26 feet 2 inches. On that day, Jesse jumped 26 feet 8 and 1/4 inches. It was a new world record!

25   In the next event, the 220-yard dash, Jesse seemed
to fly down the track. He reached the finish line in 20.3
seconds. That was another world record!

26   The last track event was the 220-yard low hurdles.
In this race, Jesse would have to run and also jump over
a series of low wooden frames. Even though he was tired
by now and his back hurt, he went on to set still another
record at 22.6 seconds.

27   After that day, Jesse Owens was famous. The newspapers began calling him "the world's fastest human."
Sports fans looked forward eagerly to the following year,
when Jesse would meet his greatest challenge as America's track star at the Olympics.

Writing Details

3. Write the name of:
   a. the girl Jesse married
   b. the university he attended
   c. the man who helped get him into the university
   d. Jesse's athletic coach at the university

4. Using complete sentences, tell:
   a. why Jesse almost missed the important track meet in Michigan
   b. in which three track events Jesse set new world records

Part III

28   **In 1936, the Olympics** played an important part in
history. The Games took place that year in Berlin, Germany. Adolf Hitler was the dictator of Germany then.
He had power over everything that happened in the
country.

29   Hitler and his followers believed that the German
people were better than everyone else, that they were a

Master Race. They boasted that Germany would soon rule the world. They believed that certain groups of people, such as Jews and blacks, were hardly human. Hitler was sure that a black athlete could never beat a German.

30   So the 1936 Olympics were not just a friendly contest between competing athletes. Hitler had turned the Games into a battle—a fight to the finish. He was sure that his German athletes would defeat all the others.

31   Jesse competed in four events: the broad jump, the 100-meter dash, the 200-meter dash, and the 400-meter relay race. The first event was the broad jump. In order to be in the broad-jump event, Jesse first had to do well in at least one out of three trials.

32   As Jesse got ready for his first trial jump, he looked at the box seat where Hitler usually sat. It was empty. Hitler had walked out on him. The German leader wouldn't stay to watch a black athlete.

33   Jesse was mad. He could feel the anger boiling inside. What had his old coach Charles Riley often told him? "An angry athlete is one who will lose every time." But Jesse couldn't help it. He was fighting mad.

34   Perhaps that was why his first jump was no good. He had been too eager to get even with Adolf Hitler. He had run down the track and started the broad jump half a foot past the takeoff board. That jump was a "foul" and didn't count.

35   The second jump was no better. This time he had not jumped far enough. Now he had only one jump left.

36   For the first time that day, Jesse felt fear rise in him. What if he didn't make the finals? Hitler would say it was because a black man wasn't good enough.

37   "What is the matter?" a voice said.

38   Jesse turned and saw Luz Long standing there. The big blue-eyed blond was Germany's best athlete. He had already easily passed the trials for the broad jump. Luz Long took Jesse by the arm.

39   "You are upset," he said. "Is it because of what Hitler did?"

40   Jesse couldn't speak. He only nodded.

41   "You are a good jumper, Jesse Owens," Luz Long went on. "You must not foul and you must jump far enough. I have been thinking. Here is what you can do. Start your last trial jump six inches *before* the takeoff board. Then jump as hard as you can."

42   Hearing these friendly words, Jesse lost his fear. More important, he had his anger under control.

43   He placed a folded towel beside the track to mark a spot six inches before the takeoff board. Down the run-

way he sped. He took off into the air. It worked! Thanks to Luz Long, he had passed the trials.

44   In each of the four events the next day, Jesse won the gold medal. He came in first in the two dashes. He led the American relay team to first place. And he beat Luz Long at the broad jump, setting a new Olympic record.

Finding the Main Idea

5. The main idea of paragraph 33 is:
   (*a*) Coach Riley used to say funny things.
   (*b*) Hitler insulted Jesse.
   (*c*) Jesse felt afraid.
   (*d*) Jesse was very angry.

6. The main idea of paragraph 44 is best expressed in sentence:
   (*a*) 1   (*b*) 2   (*c*) 3   (*d*) 4

Part IV

45   **Back in the United States,** Jesse Owens was the man of the year. His picture was in all the newspapers. Everybody wanted to see him. At a big parade for him in New York City, thousands of people stood in the streets and cheered. People gave parties in his honor. Everybody was proud of him.

46   But nobody offered Jesse a job even though he was an Olympic star. He still had one more year to go in college. He also had a wife and family to support. With less than 50 dollars in the bank, he needed a job.

47   One day, his luck seemed to change. Two men offered him a great deal of money to run races. They told him that people would pay to see Jesse Owens run against a racehorse.

48   At first he said "no." He didn't like the idea at all. But Ruth and he had two children now, and another was on the way. Also, he wanted very much to be able to finish college. So at last he agreed.

49   Three times a week, Jesse ran 100 yards against a fast racehorse. No human being can beat a racehorse, not even in a 100-yard dash, but Jesse did. How? The starter fired his gun near the horse's ear. This loud noise upset the horse so that the animal got off to a slow start. Meanwhile, Jesse raced down the track. He always won, but it was by a trick.

50   After a few months, Jesse couldn't take any more of it. He didn't feel like an athlete. He felt like an animal. One day, he quit.

51   Jobs were very hard to find in the 1930s. This was the time of the Great Depression, when many people were out of work. Jesse couldn't find a job anywhere. Once again, however, his luck seemed to change. Some men offered to put up a huge sum of money to start a chain of dry cleaning stores with him.

52   "What would I have to do?" Jesse asked.

53   "All we want is to use your name," the men said. "We want to call them the Jesse Owens Dry Cleaning Stores."

54   It seemed like a good idea. Perhaps now he would be able to finish college. He agreed to let the men use his name.

55   The stores did very well. Jesse got his college degree. He bought a large house in Cleveland for his parents and a house for his own family. At last, things were looking up for him.

56   All at once, his good luck came to an end. The men who had set up the stores abruptly left town. They also left Jesse with $50,000 in unpaid bills.

57   He decided to pay back the entire debt. To do this, he had to sell all the stores. He also had to sell both his houses. It took him five years, but he paid back all the money that was owed.

58   In the 1940s, Jesse moved his family to Detroit and then to Chicago. He earned his living by working with young people, teaching them sports. He also traveled around the country, talking to groups about the Olympic Games.

59   In 1956, the United States named Jesse "Ambassador of Sports," and sent him around the world to spread goodwill. He spoke to young people everywhere about sports and about America. He told these young people that the color of a person's skin has nothing to do with what he or she can accomplish.

60   Until his death in 1980, Jesse Owens continued to travel widely. He talked about what sports meant to him and about his belief in our country. To young people he used to say, "In America, anyone can still become somebody. That includes *you.*"

Working with Words

7. When Jesse *pleaded* (paragraph 20) with his coach, he hoped to:
   (*a*) please him   (*b*) keep his friendship
   (*c*) change his mind   (*d*) make him angry

8. A *dictator* (paragraph 28) is most like a(an):
   (*a*) athlete   (*b*) king   (*c*) speechwriter   (*d*) actor

9. to *defeat* (paragraph 30) all the other athletes, the German athletes would have to:
   (*a*) win   (*b*) lose   (*c*) boast   (*d*) cheat

10. When something is done *abruptly* (paragraph 56), it is done:
    (*a*) dishonestly   (*b*) quietly   (*c*) suddenly   (*d*) foolishly

EXERCISES

Putting Events in Sequence

A. Write the letters of each set of events in the order in which the events happened in Jesse Owens' life. For example, would you answer #1 by writing *a-b* or *b-a*? If you need help, look back at the story.

1. *a.* Charles Riley teaches Jesse to run.
   b. The Owens family moves to Cleveland, Ohio.

2. *a.* Jesse goes to Ohio State University.
   b. He marries Ruth Solomon.

3. *a.* At a track meet in Michigan, Jesse sets three new world records.
   b. Jesse takes part in the Olympic Games.

4. *a.* Jesse wins four gold medals at the Olympics.
   b. He is helped by the German athlete Luz Long.

5. *a.* Jesse pays back a debt of $50,000.
   b. The United States makes him its Ambassador of Sports.

Making Inferences

B. Use what you have read about Jesse Owens to infer, or figure out, the correct choice.

1. Which of the following is an inference?
   (*a*) Hitler didn't remain in his box seat to watch Jesse compete.
   (*b*) Hitler was furious that Jesse, a black man, won in the Olympics.
   (*c*) Hitler's best athlete helped Jesse pass the trials.
   (*d*) Hitler thought that the Germans were better than everyone else.

2. You can infer that Jesse's success as a track star made Coach Riley feel:
   (*a*) angry   (*b*) grateful   (*c*) worried   (*d*) proud

3. Jesse found himself $50,000 in debt because he was:
(*a*) too cautious   (*b*) unfamiliar with the dry cleaning business
(*c*) cheated   (*d*) unemployed

4. Which of the following was NOT an important goal for Jesse?
(*a*) getting a college education
(*b*) succeeding as an athlete
(*c*) earning a living
(*d*) succeeding in politics

Understanding Cause and Effect

   C. Write the letter of the best choice.

1. An important cause of the Owens family's move from Alabama to Ohio was:
(*a*) Jesse's poor health   (*b*) greater sports opportunities for Jesse   (*c*) the advice of Coach Riley   (*d*) the Great Depression

2. One effect of Coach Riley's help was that Jesse:
(*a*) got better grades   (*b*) could go to college
(*c*) was able to marry   (*d*) returned to Alabama

3. A likely cause of Jesse's two failures in the Olympic trials for the broad jump was:
(*a*) Jesse's anger at Hitler   (*b*) Luz Long's advice   (*c*) Jesse's sore back   (*d*) the superiority of the German athletes

4. Jesse gave up competing with a racehorse because:
(*a*) he kept losing   (*b*) it didn't pay well enough   (*c*) he felt like an animal   (*d*) his wife advised him to quit

Separating Fact from Opinion

   D. Tell which is a *fact* and which is an *opinion*.

1. On May 25, 1935, Jesse set three new world track records.

2. Coach Snyder was right to allow Jesse to enter all four track events despite Jesse's sore back.

3. Luz Long helped Jesse pass the trials.

4. Clearly, Luz Long was a kind person.

Choosing the Best Title

E. Write the number of the best title for the story of Jesse Owens.

1. He Raced Against Racehorses

2. A Track Star Who Kept Faith in America

3. The Story of the Olympics

4. Ambassador of Sports

Speaking, Listening, and Writing

G. Be prepared to discuss one of the following topics with your classmates.

1. Jesse married when he was still in high school. In today's world, how old do you think young people should be before they get married? Give reasons for your opinion.

2. What did Jesse mean when he said, "In America, anyone can still become somebody?" Do you agree with him? Tell why or why not.

H. Write a paragraph or more about one of the following topics.

1. Pretend that Luz Long and Jesse Owens were still alive. Write a letter from Jesse to Luz thanking him for his help at the Olympics. Give details of that help.

2. What do you think was the most important event in Jesse's life? Why?

3. How did Jesse show that he was brave and honorable in the years after the Olympic games?

A shy little girl becomes a famous fighter for human rights.

13. *Eleanor Roosevelt*

Part I

1   **Eleanor Roosevelt** was born in 1884 in New York City. It meant something to be born a Roosevelt. It meant that your family was one of the oldest and richest in the United States. It meant that your relatives lived in grand homes with many rooms and many servants. The Roosevelt men were leaders in banking, big business, and government. The Roosevelt women belonged to "high society."

2   Women in high society were expected to be beautiful, charming, and popular. They wore expensive dresses in the very latest fashion. Their days and nights were filled with fancy parties and dances. Eleanor's mother, Anna Roosevelt, was one of the most beautiful and popular women of her time. She felt completely at home in high society.

3   Into this world came Eleanor. As she herself once said, "I must have been a more wrinkled and less attractive baby than the average." An aunt once described her as "the ugly duckling of the family."

4   Her mother used to call her "Granny," even in front of strangers. When her mother did this, Eleanor remembered, "I wanted to sink through the floor in shame." Eleanor's beautiful mother was disappointed in her daughter, and Eleanor knew it.

5   Eleanor's childhood was full of misery. She was afraid of the dark. She was afraid of animals. She was afraid of other children. At parties, she cried so much that her mother had to take her home. At school, she did poor work.

6   "I was always disgracing my mother," Eleanor remembered.

7   But there was one person she could never disappoint or disgrace—her father. Elliott Roosevelt loved everything about his daughter. To Eleanor, he was the love of her life. When she was with her father, she was always happy.

8   Even this one happiness did not last long, for her father was a sick man. He also drank heavily. After a while, he became an alcoholic. Her parents were often unhappy together. During much of Eleanor's early childhood, her father lived far away from home.

9   Worse misery was yet to come. When Eleanor was eight years old, her mother suddenly became ill and died. Eleanor was sent to live with her grandmother. Life at her grandmother's home held no joy for Eleanor either. It was a dark and lonely place with no boys or girls her age.

10   The only bright spots in her days came with her father's letters. They were long and loving and full of advice. They held out the hope that she would grow up to be a brave, wise, and good woman. She read the letters over and over again.

11   Two years after her mother's death, her father also died. Eleanor kept his letters all her long life.

Finding Details

1. Which paragraph contains details about women in high society?
   (a) 1   (b) 2   (c) 3   (d) 4

2. In which paragraph do you learn who:
   a. once called Eleanor "the ugly duckling of the family"
   b. used to call Eleanor "Granny"
   c. took Eleanor after her mother died
   d. wrote long and loving letters to Eleanor

Part II

12 　**When Eleanor was 15** years old, she was sent to school in England for three years. She was much happier there than she had been in her grandmother's home. At school were girls her own age. She was no longer treated as someone to be pitied.

13 　The woman who ran the school liked the shy American girl. Eleanor soon became one of her favorite students. This teacher helped Eleanor to think for herself and to have faith in herself.

14 　When Eleanor returned to the United States, she needed all the help her teacher had given her. The Roosevelt family had become even more famous. Eleanor's uncle, Theodore Roosevelt, had just become President of the United States. As a young lady and a Roosevelt, Eleanor was now expected to take her place in high society.

15 　For about a year, Eleanor suffered through the parties and dances of high society. But she hated them all. They seemed empty and worthless to her.

16 　Finally, Eleanor did what *she* wanted. She stopped going to parties and dances. Instead, she joined a group called the Junior League. Working with the League, she spent her time helping poor children. She had taken one of the first steps toward becoming the real Eleanor Roosevelt.

17 　Although Eleanor was not at all pretty, she was becoming a beautiful human being. A serious and sincere

person, she cared about other people. She liked them and wanted to help them.

18   Young men began to pay attention to her. Among them was a handsome cousin of hers—Franklin Delano Roosevelt. It was not long before Franklin Roosevelt asked Eleanor Roosevelt to marry him.

19   "You won't even have to change your last name," he said jokingly.

20   The marriage of Eleanor and Franklin Roosevelt in 1905 was a big social event. President Theodore Roosevelt himself gave the bride away at the wedding. While all the guests crowded around the President, Franklin and Eleanor were content to be alone. After all, they had each other now.

21   Eleanor soon found out that Franklin and she had more than each other. There was also Franklin's growing career in politics. In 1910, he was elected to the New York State Senate. Three years later, he became Assistant Secretary of the United States Navy. In 1920, he ran for the office of Vice President of the United States, but lost. Franklin wondered if this was the end of his lifework in politics.

22   In the summer of 1921, Franklin and Eleanor Roosevelt and their children were away on vacation. Franklin, a strong and active man, had gone swimming. When he returned, he felt tired, chilled, and sick. The next day, he felt worse.

23   Eleanor was terribly worried about him. Because he was in great pain, she called in several doctors. They told her that her husband had polio—a serious, crippling disease.

24   For weeks, Eleanor nursed her husband day and night. She rubbed his legs. Since he could not move at all from the waist down, she had to lift his heavy body to sit him up.

25   "Will my husband get better?" Eleanor asked one of the doctors. "Will he be able to sit up and walk again?"

26   "It's too soon to tell," the doctor answered. "A lot depends on him. If he *wants* to lead an active life again, there is a chance. But it may take great courage and hard work for both of you."

27   Franklin would never walk again without steel leg braces and crutches. How could he hope to lead an active life? He began to lose interest in politics.

28   "What can I do to help him?" Eleanor wondered.

29   "Get him interested in politics again," an old friend advised her.

30   "How can I do that?" asked Eleanor.

31   "By going into politics yourself."

32   What a crazy idea! Shy, frightened Eleanor, the "ugly duckling" of the family, going into politics! How could she dare to do that?

33   Going into politics took all Eleanor's courage, but she did it. She began to work for the Democratic Party in New York State. She brought politicians and other important people home with her to talk to her husband. She even began to make speeches. At first, she was terrified; but with the help of friends, her speeches became better. Slowly she lost her fear.

34   Eleanor found that she enjoyed politics. More important for her, however, was that she kept her husband's name in the public eye. People admired her hard work and her husband's courage. In 1928, Franklin made his return to politics. He was elected Governor of New York State. Eleanor's hard work and faith in her husband had helped make it happen.

35   The following year, hard times hit America. Banks failed, many companies went out of business, and millions of people lost their jobs. It seemed as if the whole nation had become sick. This was the beginning of the Great Depression.

36   As the Depression grew worse, the American people wanted new leaders. They needed people with courage and new ideas. In 1932, they elected Franklin Delano Roosevelt President of the United States.

Writing Details

3. Tell how long:
  a. Eleanor went to school in England
  b. Eleanor suffered through the parties and dances of high society
  c. Franklin was out of politics (*Hint*: You'll have to figure out this answer.)

4. From the following list, write the name of each speaker.

> Eleanor Roosevelt
>
> Theodore Roosevelt
>
> Franklin Delano Roosevelt

   a. "I fell in love with and married my cousin Eleanor."

   b. "I was President of the United States when I gave my niece Eleanor away at her wedding."

   c. "I decided to join the Junior League and work with poor children."

Part III

37   **Mrs. Roosevelt was now** First Lady of the land. In the past, the wives of Presidents did little more than give parties and entertain many guests. But not Eleanor! She became the most active First Lady who ever lived in the White House.

38   Because her husband could not easily move about himself, Eleanor traveled everywhere for him. She became his eyes and ears. She visited poor coal miners in the South. She met with farmers in the West who had lost their land. She talked to hungry families in the big cities of the East. She went everywhere, and when she returned to the White House, she told her husband what she had seen and heard. She urged him to act quickly. Millions of Americans needed help right away.

39   In those days, the government did not help people who had lost their jobs. Eleanor, who cared deeply about all these people, worked closely with her husband to find ways to help them. They both tried hard to reach out to all Americans. Eleanor wrote daily articles for the newspapers about life in the White House. She called the articles "My Day." Even the Roosevelts' little black dog Fala was known to everyone. President Roosevelt often talked over the radio in friendly "fireside chats" to the nation. People liked and trusted their President, whom they

Eleanor Roosevelt (center) at Hyde Park, NY.

called "FDR," and they began to feel close to him and his family.

40   On December 7, 1941, America was swept into World War II. The United States joined many other nations to fight against Germany, Italy, and Japan. Before the war, Eleanor's work had taken her all over the country. Now her new duties took her all over the world. With her own eyes, she saw the full horrors of war. Someday, she told herself, she would try to find a way to end war.

41   Only a few months before the end of the war, FDR suddenly died. He had been elected President for four terms, and he had been in office longer than any other American President. The people felt that they had lost a great leader.

42   Mrs. Roosevelt called the Vice President, Harry Truman, to the White House. He would now become the new President.

43   "Is there anything I can do for you?" he asked Eleanor.

44   Harry Truman never forgot her quiet, thoughtful answer.

45   "Is there anything *we* can do for you?" she said. "For *you* are the one in trouble now."

Finding the Main Idea

5. The main idea of paragraph 39 is:
   (*a*) The government did not help people who were out of work.
   (*b*) FDR talked to the people on the radio.
   (*c*) FDR and Eleanor reached out to all Americans.
   (*d*) The American people called their President "FDR."

6. The main idea of Part III is:
   (*a*) As First Lady, Eleanor did a great deal for America.
   (*b*) Franklin D. Roosevelt was a wonderful President.
   (*c*) The Great Depression put people out of work.
   (*d*) World War II caused much pain and suffering.

Part IV

46   **After the death** of her husband, Eleanor returned to private life in New York. She had been First Lady of the land for more than 12 years. She was 61 years old.

47   "What will you do now?" the newspaper reporters asked her.

48   "The story is over," Eleanor said.

49   But the story was far from over. For 17 more years, Mrs. Roosevelt went on working for a better life for people everywhere.

50   After World War II ended, the United Nations was

formed. The first meeting was to be in London, England. One day, President Truman called Eleanor.

51   "I want you to serve with the Americans at the first United Nations meeting," he said.

52   "I couldn't possibly do that," she replied. "I have never worked in foreign affairs. I would be of no use dealing with people of other nations at such a meeting."

53   President Truman insisted, however, and Eleanor finally agreed. At the United Nations, she found herself in the middle of a fierce fight.

54   During the war, many people had been forced to flee from their countries. The Russians had taken over some of these countries. Now the Russians said all the people who ran away must return to their homes. But many of them didn't want to go back and live under Russian control.

55   At the United Nations meeting, the man who spoke for the Russians made a strong and angry speech. Since the Americans at the meeting wanted no trouble with the Russians, they didn't know how to answer this man—but Mrs. Roosevelt did.

56   Speaking with great feeling, she defended the right of people to be free. It was clear to all that she cared deeply about people, and this made her listeners care as well. The members of the United Nations voted against the Russians.

57   Eleanor had been afraid she would be of no use at the United Nations. Instead, she was the only American who dared to stand up for freedom and human rights.

58   An even more important task lay ahead of her. The members of the United Nations had decided to write a "Declaration of Human Rights." It would state their belief that all human beings should be free—that all must have human rights. President Truman again asked Eleanor to go to the United Nations. There the members, who came from many different nations of the world, elected Eleanor to lead them.

59   It took two years of hard work for the members to agree on what to say in the Declaration. Without Eleanor Roosevelt as their leader, they might never have agreed. In 1948, the entire United Nations voted to accept the "Declaration of Human Rights."

60   For many years, Eleanor had been the First Lady of the United States. Now she was often called the "First Lady of the World." To many people, she seemed even larger than life.

61   They tell the story of the mother who took her small child to see the Statue of Liberty.

62   "Do you know who that is, dear?" the mother asked.

63   The child looked up at the huge statue of a woman.

64   "Sure," the child said. "That's Mrs. Roosevelt."

65   In 1962, Eleanor Roosevelt died. Men, women, and children all over the world felt that they had lost a great and good friend. The shy and frightened little girl of long ago had become a woman of strength and courage. Adlai Stevenson, an old friend, described her spirit best. He said, "She would rather light a candle than curse the darkness, and her glow has warmed the world."

Working with Words

7. In the expression "high society," the word *high* (paragraph 1) refers to:
   (*a*) being tall
   (*b*) feeling happy
   (*c*) living on a hill
   (*d*) belonging to the upper class

8. The *expensive* (paragraph 2) dresses worn by women in high society must have been:
   (*a*) tight-fitting   (*b*) high-priced
   (*c*) colorful   (*d*) covered with jewels

9. A *sincere* (paragraph 17) person is best described as:
(*a*) peaceful   (*b*) caring   (*c*) deceitful   (*d*) honest

10. Use the following list of related words to write the missing words below.

politics (paragraph 21)
politician
political

a. Eleanor never thought that she could be a _____.
b. She gave _____ speeches to help her husband.
c. With her help, Franklin returned to _____.

EXERCISES

Putting Events in Sequence

A.   Write the letters of each set of events in the order in which the events happened in Eleanor Roosevelt's life. For example, would you answer #1 by writing *a-b* or *b-a*? If you need help, look back at the story.

1. *a.* Eleanor is sent to school in England.
   b. Her parents both die.

2. *a.* Her uncle Theodore Roosevelt becomes President of the United States.
   b. She marries Franklin Delano Roosevelt.

3. *a.* She goes into politics.
   b. Franklin is crippled by polio and cannot walk.

4. *a.* Franklin is elected President of the United States.
   b. In wartime, Eleanor travels all over the world.

5. *a.* Eleanor leads the United Nations group that writes the "Declaration of Human Rights."
   b. Franklin dies.

Making Inferences

B.   Use what you have read about Eleanor Roosevelt to infer, or figure out, the correct choice.

1. The person who probably had the most positive influence upon Eleanor was her:
   (*a*) mother
   (*b*) father
   (*c*) grandmother
   (*d*) Uncle Theodore Roosevelt

2. Eleanor's remark to Harry Truman (paragraph 45) immediately after her husband's death reveals her:
   (*a*) grief   (*b*) pride   (*c*) understanding   (*d*) resentment

3. You can infer that the members of the United Nations admired Mrs. Roosevelt for:
   (*a*) her courage
   (*b*) her patriotism
   (*c*) her devotion to her husband
   (*d*) all of the above

4. Eleanor's true interest in life could best be described as:
   (*a*) politics   (*b*) high society
   (*c*) pleasing her mother   (*d*) helping other people

Understanding Cause and Effect

C.   Write the letter of the best choice.

1. One effect of the three years Eleanor spent at school in England was to give her:
   (*a*) lifelong friends   (*b*) useful contacts
   (*c*) a British accent   (*d*) greater self-confidence

2. The chief cause of Eleanor's first becoming involved in politics was:
   (*a*) her mother's wishes   (*b*) her own ambition
   (*c*) her husband's illness   (*c*) Harry Truman's advice

3. As First Lady, Eleanor traveled throughout America and all over the world to be able to report back to:

(*a*) Harry Truman   (*b*) her husband

(*c*) Theodore Roosevelt   (*d*) the United Nations

4. As a result of Eleanor's work at the United Nations, member nations have agreed to:

(*a*) avoid war

(*b*) respect human rights

(*c*) develop nuclear arms

(*d*) stop spying on other nations

Separating Fact from Opinion

D. Tell which is a *fact* and which is an *opinion.*

1. Both Eleanor's parents died before she was 15.

2. Franklin and Eleanor had a happy marriage.

3. Eleanor was First Lady for more than 12 years.

4. After her husband's death, Eleanor served at the United Nations.

Choosing the Best Title

E. Write the number of the best title for the story of Eleanor Roosevelt.

1. Daughter of Presidents

2. Friend of Humanity

3. Lady of High Society

4. Leader at the United Nations

Speaking, Listening, and Writing

    F. Make some notes to yourself on one of the following topics, so that you could talk briefly about the topic if called upon by your teacher. (If you need help, look back at the story.)

1. What were some of the things that Eleanor Roosevelt did as First Lady?

2. What people or events in Eleanor's life do you think helped her become such a brave and kind woman?

    G. Write a paragraph or more on one of the following topics. (You may wish to make up a name for the real person you choose to write about.)

1. Tell about someone you know or know about who had a difficult childhood but turned out well.

2. Tell about someone you know or know about who overcame shyness or some other fear.

3. Write an invitation to Eleanor, as if she were still alive, to visit your class and talk about the most important deed she did in her life. Explain which deed you'd like her to talk about and why.

A brave priest builds missions in California.

14. Junípero Serra

Part I

1   **Father Junípero Serra** was born in 1713 in Majorca, an island off the coast of Spain. His parents were farmers, plain folk who could not read or write. They named their baby boy Miguel.

2   As a young boy, Miguel Serra was sent to a nearby school run by Franciscan monks. The Franciscans are members of a Catholic religious order who live by the teachings of Saint Francis. This saint taught his followers to lead lives that are simple, pure, and full of love for all living things.

3   When he was almost 16, Miguel joined the Franciscan Order. He liked to read books about Franciscans who had gone to the New World. (In those days, North America and South America were called the New World.) He longed to go the New World; work among the native people there, called Indians; and lead them into Christianity. This became his dream.

4   In time, Miguel became a priest. He changed his first name to Junípero in honor of a special friend and follower of Saint Francis. For many years, Father Serra studied and then taught at the university in Palma, the chief city of Majorca. As a teacher at the school, he was famous and respected.

5   Two of his students, Father Palou and Father Crespi, became his friends. They were sure that a bright future

lay ahead for their friend and teacher. To Father Serra, however, fame and a high position in the Church meant nothing. He had never forgotten his early desire. In 1748, when he was 35 years old, he asked to be sent to the New World to work among the Indians there.

6   Fathers Palou and Crespi could hardly believe the news. Why would anyone give up a great future to face hardships and dangers in a strange land far across the ocean?

7   "If you are really going," the two friends said to Father Serra, "then we will go with you."

8   Tears of joy filled Father Serra's eyes. Taking off his eyeglasses, he wiped his eyes. He smiled at the two younger men.

9   "I thank God," he said. "Now I shall have the company of my dearest friends in that distant land."

Finding Details

1. Give the number of the paragraph that tells:
   a. where Father Serra taught school
   b. who the Franciscans are
   c. when Father Serra asked to be sent to the New World
   d. what his two friends said to him

2. In which two paragraphs do you learn why Father Serra wanted to go to the New World?
   (a) 1 and 4   (b) 2 and 6   (c) 3 and 5   (d) 4 and 9

Part II

10   **In those days**, over 200 years ago, travel was slow and difficult. The trip from Spain across the Atlantic Ocean to Mexico, which then belonged to Spain, took

100 days. At last, however, the ship landed in the port of Vera Cruz in Mexico. Father Palou became sick there. Since Father Crespi wanted to stay with him until he felt better, Father Serra decided to go ahead to their final goal, Mexico City.

11   It was a rule of the Franciscan Order that its members must not ride a horse or a mule unless they had to. Father Serra therefore made up his mind to walk the entire 250 miles. Another priest went with him.

12   Near the end of the long trip, Father Serra had an accident. As he slept on the ground one night, a scorpion stung his left leg. (A scorpion is a small, poisonous animal related to the spider.) By morning, the leg was so badly swollen that Father Serra could hardly walk. Slowly, he limped the last few miles into Mexico City.

13   The wound on his leg never healed. For the rest of his life, he was lame and often in great pain.

14   Father Serra spent the next 19 years working in and around Mexico City. For many years, Father Palou and he lived with an unusually poor tribe of Indians called the Pames. Their home was in the Sierra Gorda hills, about 200 miles from Mexico City.

15   Father Serra learned the language of the Pames. Then he worked with the men to plant corn and raise sheep and cows. He worked with the women to spin cloth and weave baskets. In a few years, the Pames were no longer poor.

16   During this time, the King of Spain began to fear that Russia or England might try to take over California. He decided to claim the land for Spain. To do this, he would have to send Spanish soldiers, priests, and settlers into California.

17   The soldiers would build forts to keep out the Russians and the English. The forts would also protect the Spanish people from attacks by Indians.

18   The priests would set up missions. Each mission would have a church as well as a farm to grow food. By

working on the farm, the Indians would learn how to grow crops and raise sheep and cows. These missions would be like the one Father Serra had founded among the Pame Indians of Sierra Gorda.

19   Finally, Spanish settlers—men, women, and children—would come to farm and to build towns. In this way, the King felt, California would surely belong to Spain.

20   Only the bravest and best leaders could carry out such a plan. Father Serra was chosen to set up a chain of missions. They would stretch from Mexico far up into California.

Writing Details

3. From the following list, write the places that are mentioned in this part of the story.

    Spain   Mexico   England   Italy
    France   Russia   Majorca   California

4. Answer these questions.
    a. How long did it take to go from Spain to Mexico in Father Serra's time?
    b. How far was it from Vera Cruz to Mexico City?
    c. For how many years did Father Serra work in and around Mexico City?

Part III

21   **In 1769, two groups** of Spanish soldiers and priests left on foot from Mexico and headed for California. Captain Portola, who led one overland group, was to be the military commander of California. He would be in charge of the soldiers and the forts. Captain Rivera, who

led the other group, was to be his second-in-command. As these two groups headed north, the sun shone brightly on the steel helmets of the soldiers. Their guns made long black shadows on the ground.

22   They were all headed for San Diego, California. From there they would go farther north to Monterey. Father Serra was to join Captain Portola's party on the way to San Diego.

23   Early one spring morning, Father Serra said good-bye to Father Palou. The younger man had been or-dered to remain, for the time being, in Mexico. When Father Palou saw the swelling and terrible sores on his friend's left leg, tears came to his eyes.

24   "I have never seen you so sick before," he said. "Let me go in your place. I am afraid this long trip will kill you."

25   "No," Father Serra replied. "I have put my trust in God, and He will help me."

26   Two men had to lift Father Serra onto the saddle of his old mule. The little group moved slowly off with Father Serra and two soldiers in the lead. Behind them came the pack mules and the mule driver.

27   Day after day, they traveled north into California. They crossed wide, empty deserts and climbed over

steep mountains. By day, they marched in the heat of the sun. By night, they heard the sounds of wild animals all around them.

28   The pain in Father Serra's leg grew worse, until he was simply unable to go on. He called the mule driver to him.

29   "Tell me, my son," Father Serra said. "Can you do anything to help my leg?"

30   The mule driver scratched his head. "But, Father, I am not a doctor," the man said. "I am only a driver of mules. I know how to help the mules when they are sick, but that is all."

31   A smile appeared on Father Serra's round face. Behind his eyeglasses, his eyes were merry with good humor.

32   "Treat me as one of your mules," he said. "Do for me what you would do for a mule if it had a sore leg."

33   The mule driver made some medicine and put it on Father Serra's leg. For the first time in many nights, Father Serra slept well. The next morning, his leg felt better, and he could go on.

34   After many days of travel, Father Serra caught up with Captain Portola and his men. The Captain was glad to see the priest. He liked him, and they got along well. Both men were happy to be traveling together through the wild country.

35   They began to see Indians along the way. Some were friendly. They brought gifts of food to the travelers. They asked for clothing, pieces of cloth, or other strange things belonging to the travelers.

36   One day, about 40 Indians appeared in front of them and made signs for them to turn back. The Indians shouted something angrily. Clearly, they did not want these strangers in their land. Shaking their fists, the Indians came closer.

37   Captain Portola gave an order to his men. The

Spanish soldiers fired their guns into the air. The thunder of the guns and the clouds of black smoke frightened the Indians, who turned and fled. Father Serra looked sadly after them.

38   "Guns are not the way to make friends with people," he said. "We can do that only with love."

39   At last they reached San Diego. Captain Rivera and his men were already there. When two ships brought much-needed supplies, the men could begin work on the fort and the mission.

40   On a hill near the ocean, Father Serra built the first of his missions. He named it Mission San Diego de Alcala. The Spanish soldiers made huts of branches and brushwood. The largest of the huts became the church. Later, they would build better houses and a fine church of stone.

41   The soldiers put up a tall wooden cross. Father Serra blessed it. High in a tree, they hung a large bell. As Father Serra rang the bell, he sang a song of joy and thanksgiving to God. The ringing of the bell and the loud, clear voice of Father Serra brought curious Indians to the Mission. When Father Serra saw them, his round face beamed with love.

42   "At last," he said, "I can begin the work I have traveled so far to do."

43   An Indian boy who spoke Spanish had come with them from Mexico to serve as a translator. He helped Father Serra talk to the Indians. Slowly Father Serra began to learn some of their language. He wanted to win their trust and friendship.

44   Leaving two priests and some soldiers to take care of the mission in San Diego, Captain Portola and Father Serra led the rest of the Spanish soldiers and priests farther north to Monterey. There Father Serra built his second mission, San Carlos de Monterey. Soon another church bell was ringing in California.

Finding the Main Idea

5. The main idea of paragraph 21 is stated in sentence:
   (*a*) 1   (*b*) 2   (*c*) 4   (*d*) 5

6. The main idea of paragraphs 39–44 is:
   (*a*) supplying the missions by ship
   (*b*) working with the Indians
   (*c*) building the first two missions in California
   (*d*) blessing the cross and ringing the bell

Part IV

45   **Father Serra had bravely** faced dangers and suffered great pain. For many more years, however, he would find no peace. This time his worst problems were caused by his own people.

46   A new man was put in command of the soldiers in California. This man was Captain Rivera. The Captain was not only strict, but also cruel. He hated California and wanted only to return to Mexico. He did not like or trust the Indians, and he cared nothing about building new missions.

47   Early in November 1775, a number of Indians who lived near San Diego attacked the mission. They feared that the Spanish priests and soldiers would soon control all of them. The Indians did not want to lose their freedom. They burned the buildings and killed several people. Among the dead was the mission priest.

48   When Father Serra heard the news, he grieved deeply. Despite his great sorrow over the deaths, he begged Captain Rivera to show mercy to the Indians of San Diego.

49   "Mercy and love are the Christian way," he said. "Do not seek revenge."

50   Captain Rivera would not listen. With his soldiers, he rode to San Diego to punish the Indians. The soldiers caught some of the Indians and beat them almost to death. Father Serra felt sickened by the Captain's harsh action.

51   For a long time, Father Serra had hoped to build a mission in the north. He planned to call this new mission by the Spanish name for Saint Francis. Despite Captain Rivera, Father Serra's dearest dream finally came true. In 1776, a mission was started far to the north. It was named San Francisco.

52   By 1782, Father Serra had founded nine missions, stretching from San Francisco in the north down to San Diego in the south. Father Palou was in charge of the mission in San Francisco. Father Serra and Father Crespi lived and worked together in the mission at Monterey.

53   Thousands of Indians, many of whom had become Christians, lived in these missions. They learned how to grow grain and how to raise pigs and cattle. They planted orange and olive trees and grapevines.

54   Father Serra was almost 70 years old. Pains in his chest and his sore leg made travel very hard. Yet in the last year of his life, he traveled hundreds of miles to visit all nine of his missions.

55   He died peacefully in Monterey in August 1784. No one had played a more important part in the Spanish settlement of California. Perhaps no other person had worked so well with the Indians as Father Junípero Serra had done.

56   How sad the good Father would have been if he could have known what was to happen! The Indians who had helped to farm so much land in California faced a terrible future.

57   Mexico broke away from Spain in 1822 and became a separate country. About 10 years later, the missions were closed, and their lands were sold to private owners.

Thousands of Indians who had lived and worked in the missions were left homeless.

58   In 1848, as a result of the Mexican-American War, the United States took California away from Mexico. One year later, gold was discovered in California. Americans rushed there to look for gold, and many stayed to farm and build towns.

59   As more new settlers moved into California, the Indians were pushed from place to place. They were forced to live in special areas called reservations. These were usually on worthless land that could not be farmed. Even today, many Indians are still poor and angry strangers in their own land.

60   What happened to the Indians of California would have broken the heart of Father Serra, a man as kind and loving as he was brave.

Statue of Father Serra in San Francisco, CA.

61   Today, three large statues honor him. One statue stands in Golden Gate Park in San Francisco. A second one stands in front of the beautiful old mission of Capistrano. A third statue can be seen in the Capitol building in Washington, D.C. On the base of this statue are only three words: *Junípero Serra—California.*

62   Recognizing his "life of heroic virtue," Pope John Paul II declared Father Serra "venerable" in 1985. Three years later, the Pope beatified him, or declared him "blessed." Some day, Father Serra may exceed even the expectations of his dear friends Fathers Palou and Crespi by being canonized as a saint.

Working with Words

7. In paragraph 2, the word *order* most nearly means:
(*a*) group   (*b*) command   (*c*) arrangement   (*d*) writing

8. A *military* (paragraph 21) commander would be responsible for:
(*a*) civilians   (*b*) public schools   (*c*) factories   (*d*) soldiers

9. A *translator* (paragraph 43) is one who:
(*a*) lives in more than one country
(*b*) speaks two or more languages
(*c*) wins the trust and friendship of others
(*d*) teaches languages in a school

10. Use the following list of related words to write the missing words below.
> grieved (paragraph 48)
> grief
> grievous

a. Father Serra heard the _____ news of the attack on the mission.
b. He _____ for those who had died.
c. Despite his _____, he wanted no part of revenge.

EXERCISES

Putting Events in Sequence

A. Write the letters of each set of events in the order in which the events happened in the story of Father Serra. For example, would you answer #1 by writing *a-b* or *b-a*? If you need help, look back at the story.

1. *a.* Father Serra goes to the New World to work among the Indians.
   b. He teaches at the University of Palma.

2. *a.* He is stung on the leg by a scorpion.
   b. He lives and works with the Pames.

3. *a.* From Mexico, he travels overland to San Diego, California.
   b. Captain Rivera replaces Captain Portola.

4. *a.* The mission of San Francisco is built in the North.
   b. Indians attack the mission at San Diego.

5. *a.* Father Serra dies at Monterey.
   b. The missions are closed, and many Indians are left homeless.

Making Inferences

B. Use what you have learned about Father Serra to infer, or figure out, the correct choice.

1. You can infer that Father Serra's native language was:
   (*a*) English   (*b*) Spanish   (*c*) Latin   (*d*) French

2. At the sight of Father Serra's infected leg, Father Palou shed tears of:
   (*a*) pity   (*b*) disgust   (*c*) disappointment   (*d*) anger

3. From the part of the story about the mule medicine (paragraphs 28–33), you can infer that Father Serra:
   (*a*) was not proud   (*b*) had a sense of humor
   (*c*) was very practical   (*d*) all of the above

4. If someone were to hurt Father Serra, he would probably:
   (*a*) fight back angrily   (*b*) forgive the person
   (*c*) seek revenge   (*d*) run away in terror

Understanding Cause and Effect

C. Write the letter of the correct choice.

1. Father Serra was lame in one leg because of a (an):
   (*a*) fall   (*b*) Indian attack
   (*c*) scorpion bite   (*d*) childhood disease

2. One effect of Father Serra's work with the Pames of Mexico was that they:
   (*a*) moved to California
   (*b*) learned Spanish
   (*c*) improved their lives
   (*d*) stopped fighting with their neighbors

3. At San Diego, the Spaniards were able to set to work building a fort and a mission because:
   (*a*) the Indians agreed to help
   (*b*) supply ships arrived
   (*c*) the rains finally stopped
   (*d*) Captain Portola's soldiers protected them

4. The great gold rush to California in 1849 proved bad for the:
   (*a*) Mexicans   (*b*) Americans   (*c*) Spaniards   (*d*) Indians

Separating Fact from Opinion

D. Tell which is a *fact* and which is an *opinion*.

1. If Father Serra had not chosen to go to the New World, he would certainly have risen to a high position in the Church.

2. Father Serra built nine missions in California.

3. During Father Serra's lifetime, Mexico belonged to Spain.

4. It would have been better if Father Serra had left the Indians of California alone.

Choosing the Best Title

E.   Write the number of the best title for the story of Father Serra.

1. The Proud Priest

2. A Traveler in Mexico

3. Builder of Missions

4. An Explorer in America

Speaking, Listening, and Writing

F.   Be prepared to discuss one of the following topics.

1. How did Father Serra show that he was a brave man?
2. How did Father Serra show that he was a kind man?

G.   Write a paragraph or more about one of the following topics.

1. What were the missions in California, and how were they used?
2. What do you know about the early history of your community? Which Native Americans—if any—lived there? Which Europeans first settled there, and when?
3. What do you think was the bravest thing that Father Serra did? In a brief article for your school newspaper, explain your answer.

A dying schoolteacher finds a new life helping the mentally ill.

15. Dorothea Lynde Dix

Part I

1   **About a hundred years ago** in America, most mentally ill people led miserable lives. They were thrown into jails, locked away in cells, or chained in cages. Thousands of insane men and women spent their lives sick, starved, filthy, and forgotten.

2   To change all this was the lifework of one woman. For more than 40 years, Dorothea Lynde Dix fought for better treatment of the mentally ill.

3   Perhaps her concern for the poor and sick of mind came from her own childhood. Her early years were so hard and sad that it pained her to remember them.

4   "What was your childhood like?" somebody once asked Dorothea when she was a grown woman.

5   "I had no childhood," was her reply.

6   Her father, Joseph Dix, was the son of a wealthy family of Boston, Massachusetts. At the age of 18, Joseph married a poor farm woman almost twice his age. The young man became a wandering preacher. He began to speak and act strangely, as if his mind were troubled. In 1802, a baby girl was born. Joseph named the baby after his mother—Dorothea Lynde Dix.

7   They were not a happy family. Dorothea's mother was usually sick and complaining. Her father was often away, either preaching or drinking in a tavern. In the dirty, run-down house, the little girl heard many angry words.

8   Dorothea learned to cook meals. She cleaned the house. Often she nursed her sick mother. In addition, she had to spend long hours cutting and pasting and sewing together the loose pages of her father's printed sermons. Two younger brothers were born, and she also had to take care of them.

9   At the age of 12, Dorothea was taken to live with her stern grandmother in Boston. Grandmother Dix decided to make a lady out of Dorothea. She bought her fancy dresses, which Dorothea disliked. She made her take dancing lessons, which Dorothea hated. She forced her to spend long hours learning to do fine needlework. To Dorothea, this seemed as bad as sewing the pages of her father's sermons. No wonder Dorothea felt that she never had a childhood!

10   Dorothea was not content to be just a lady. She wanted to do something useful with her life. In those days, more than a hundred years ago, only boys went to public school. If girls went to school at all, they went to private schools. When Dorothea was only 14, she decided to start a small private school for girls.

11   She had little formal education herself. She read a great deal, however, and she was clever and hardworking. To prepare herself for teaching, she started working at five o'clock each morning, reading books and studying. She rarely stopped working before midnight.

12   Dorothea met the famous Boston minister Dr. William Ellery Channing. He was a social reformer, a man who worked to improve the lives of others. He preached God's love for all living beings. Dr. Channing became Dorothea's close friend, and he encouraged her in her work.

13   For almost 20 years, Dorothea taught school. She wrote eight books for children, some of them very popular. Studying, teaching, writing from early morning to late at night, she drove herself too hard.

14   Her health began to break down. Long, painful fits of coughing were followed by fever and weakness. After a while, she was coughing up blood. She had tuberculosis, a disease of the lungs.

15   Dorothea had to close her school because she was too sick to teach. She was only 34, but she felt that her life's work was over.

16   Actually, she had no need to work. Her grandmother died, leaving her a great deal of money. Also, she had some income from the sale of her books. She could have spent the rest of her life, quiet, comfortable, and unknown. Five years after closing her school, however, when she was 39, Dorothea's life changed suddenly and dramatically.

Finding Details

1. Dorothea's illness is described in paragraph:
   (*a*) 8   (*b*) 11   (*c*) 13   (*d*) 14

2. Which paragraph tells Dorothea's age when:
   a. she went to live with her grandmother
   b. she opened a school for girls
   c. illness forced her to close her school
   d. her life changed suddenly

Part II

17   **One day, Dorothea** heard that poor, insane people were kept in a jail just outside Boston. She decided to visit the jail. It was a chilly and windy Sunday morning in March 1841. Snow and slush covered the ground.

18   "I have been told the insane are kept here," Dorothea said to the jailer. "Please let me see them."

19   The jailer looked in surprise at the tall, well-dressed woman.

20   "It's no place for a lady," he said. "Matter of fact, nobody goes there unless they have to."

21   "I will go there anyway," she said in a low, firm voice.

22   The jailer obeyed her. He led her out to the prison yard. In the frozen ground was a heavy trapdoor. Lifting it and lighting a lantern, the jailer climbed down into a dark, cold cave. With a shudder, she followed him.

23   There Dorothea saw things that she would never forget. Thin, dirty men and women dressed in rags sat on wet, foul-smelling straw. They were chained to the rough stone walls. Screams and groans filled the air. In the freezing cold, Dorothea shivered.

24   Filled with horror and pity, she remembered the troubled life of her father. She went to see her friend, Dr. Channing, to tell him what she had seen in the jail.

25   "How can people be so cruel to the insane?" she asked the minister.

26   "Most people are not cruel," he said. "They are only ignorant. They do not know how badly the insane are treated. Somebody must teach them the facts."

27   Dorothea smiled sadly. "I was once a teacher," she said.

28   "Perhaps you must become a different kind of teacher."

29   "Why should the insane be kept in jails?" she went on. "All over Massachusetts, they must suffer as they do here in Boston. What can be done to help them?"

30   "The state must build a large hospital for the insane," Dr. Channing said. "Money must be raised. New laws must be passed. The people of Massachusetts will do this only when they know the facts."

31   Armed with a pen and a notebook, Dorothea set out to collect the facts. During the next year and a half, she visited over 500 towns and villages from one end of Massachusetts to the other.

32   Wherever she went, she asked to see where the insane were kept. She was taken to jails, to dusty attics, to dark cellars, even to wooden cages out in the fields. What she saw almost broke her heart. But in her notebook, she wrote only the facts:

Town of Lincoln—a woman caged
Town of Franklin—a man in chains
Town of Medford—man in a stall for 17 years
Town of Newton—man without legs, chained

33   In 1843, she gave a report of what she had seen to the Massachusetts state lawmakers. She called her report a "Memorial." In it, she told the lawmakers about "the present state of the insane, persons locked in cages, closets, cellars, stalls, pens, chained, naked, beaten with rods and lashed."

34   The lawmakers were shocked. At first, they didn't want to believe her. When Dorothea also wrote the facts for the newspapers, however, the people of Massachusetts believed her, and they wrote angry letters to their lawmakers. At last, the lawmakers voted money to build a large hospital in Worcester for the insane. Dorothea had won her first battle for the mentally ill.

Writing Details

3. How did Dr. Channing explain what seemed to be the cruelty of people to the insane?

4. Tell what four things Dr. Channing said must be done to help the insane.

Part III

35   **In New Jersey,** Dorothea prepared another Memorial. It told of the 500 insane persons she had visited in the state. There were the same sad stories as in Massachusetts. She asked the lawmakers to vote $150,000 to build a model hospital for the mentally ill, but they only laughed at her. In those days, that was a large sum of money.

36   Dorothea was not discouraged. Remembering what Dr. Channing had told her, she understood that these men were only ignorant, that she would have to teach them. She invited each of the lawmakers to visit her in the lobby of the hotel where she was staying. On those cold, windy February evenings they came, sometimes alone, sometimes in groups.

37   She didn't make speeches to them. She never argued with them. Instead, she spoke simply and quietly of what she had seen. She told them of insane people locked in tiny sheds and dark cellars. She described men and women who shivered without heat or blankets or even clothing.

38   "Gentlemen," she said, "you sit here in your heavy winter clothes, next to the warm stove. Yet this very evening, many of these mentally ill people of New Jersey will freeze to death."

39   Her facts changed the minds of the lawmakers. More important, though, her gentle manner moved their hearts. Almost all of them voted for the new model hospital.

40   Dorothea chose a place near Trenton, New Jersey, for the new hospital. It would be built high on a hill, overlooking the Delaware River. In this light, clean building, mentally ill men and women would be cared for with understanding and love.

41   In 1845, Dorothea set out to study the treatment of the mentally ill all over the country. For three and a half years, she bravely faced the hardships of travel across the wild, unsettled West. Only a few years before, she had been sick and expecting to die. The doctors who had given her up as hopeless had not known of her inner strength. Her will was like steel.

42   To a friend, she wrote: "I have traveled more than 10 thousand miles. I have visited 18 state penitentiaries; 300 county jails and houses of correction; more than 500 poorhouses, hospitals, and houses of refuge."

43   From the West, she moved on through the South. In state after state, she presented her Memorials. Almost always, she worked and begged and succeeded all by herself. Once, however, she had unexpected help.

44   In North Carolina, the hearts of the lawmakers were like stones. None of them would help her. In Raleigh, the capital city, she read her Memorial aloud to them. Although the lawmakers listened politely, they would not vote any money to build a state hospital.

45   Feeling beaten and alone, Dorothea returned to her hotel. As she walked slowly down the hall, she heard the sound of moaning. It came from an open door. She stepped inside and found a sick woman lying in the hotel bed. All afternoon, Dorothea nursed the sick woman. In the evening, a man appeared.

46   "Who are you?" he asked.

47   "I am Dorothea Dix. I heard this poor woman moaning and stayed to help her. Who are you?"

48   "I am her husband. My name is James Dobbin. My wife and I are here in Raleigh because of my work. My wife is very sick, but she would not let me leave her back home."

49   Mrs. Dobbin was dying of tuberculosis. This was the same disease that had almost killed Dorothea. For weeks, she nursed Mrs. Dobbin while her husband was at work. Finally, the sick woman died. Dorothea went with James Dobbin to his wife's funeral in their hometown. Soon afterward, James Dobbin said he must go back to the state capital at Raleigh.

50   "My wife spoke to me of you and your good work, Miss Dix," he said. "Now I must return to my own work."

51   Just before the Christmas holiday, James Dobbin, state lawmaker, stood up among his fellow lawmakers of North Carolina. On his arm, he wore a black band of mourning. In a low but clear voice, he spoke of his beloved wife. He described Dorothea Dix's tender care.

52   "I am here today, gentlemen," he said, "to ask you to vote money for the new hospital. It was my wife's dying wish."

53   There was a long silence. Then the voting began. On that day, the lawmakers voted "yes." The new hospital would be built after all.

Finding the Main Idea

5. The main idea of paragraph 35 is best expressed in sentence:
   (a) 1   (b) 2   (c) 3   (d) 4

6. Match the letter of each main idea with the letter of the paragraph numbers in Part III containing that main idea.
   a. Dorothea's work in the West   a. 35–40
   b. Her work in New Jersey   b. 44–53
   c. Her work in North Carolina   c. 41–42

Part IV

54   **By 1848, Dorothea** had visited 30 states. In each one, she had gathered facts about the needs of the insane. She had worked long and hard, but the need was still great. All over America, there were more than 22,000 insane people. The state hospitals could care for fewer than 4000 patients.

55   Dorothea saw that she could not help enough by working in each state. The job was too big. She would have to turn to the national government in Washington, D.C.

56   Her plan was a simple one. The national government owned many millions of acres of land all over the country. By selling about 12 million acres, the government could raise enough money to build hospitals for all the mentally ill.

57   For six years, Dorothea worked behind the scenes in Washington. Five times the lawmakers voted against her plan. At last, they voted for it. But then President Franklin Pierce refused to approve the plan.

58   The President believed that each state should take care of its poor mentally ill people. If the national government took over this job, he said, it would soon be expected to take care of all poor people. He feared that this would tend to weaken the power of the states and give too much power to the national government.

59   Dorothea's six years of work had failed. She was sick at heart. Moreover, the work and strain had made her old illness worse. By now she was almost 60 years old. Hadn't she done enough? Wasn't it time for her to rest?

60   In 1861, the Civil War broke out. At once, Dorothea offered to help. In June 1861, President Lincoln made her Superintendent of Army Nurses. She set up hospitals for the wounded soldiers, and she helped collect medicine and other supplies. She also found and trained young women to serve as nurses.

61   After the war, she returned to her lifelong concern for the mentally ill. Year after year, she visited the many mental hospitals she had helped build before the war.

62   At last, she became too old and weak to travel. She went to live in an apartment built just for her on the top floor of the state mental hospital at Trenton, New Jersey. Famous visitors from all over the world came to see her. In 1887, she died there at the age of 85.

63   More than 50 years earlier, illness had overtaken Dorothea. She had thought then that her life and work were done. But her concern for others proved stronger than her illness.

64   Thanks to Dorothea Dix, mentally ill people are not treated as criminals today. They are treated as human beings who need help. This quiet, gentle schoolteacher taught the world a lesson of courage and love.

Working with Words

7. A person who is *insane* (paragraph 1) can best be described as:
   (*a*) unclean   (*b*) immoral   (*c*) mentally ill   (*d*) physically ill

8. You would expect a *reformer* (paragraph 12) to try to:
   (*a*) change people   (*b*) avoid people
   (*c*) keep things the same   (*d*) become rich

9. In paragraph 26, the work *ignorant* means:
   (*a*) able to teach the facts
   (*b*) willing to learn the facts
   (*c*) unwilling to accept the facts
   (*d*) unaware of the facts

10. A black band of *mourning* (paragraph 51) is a symbol of:
    (*a*) one who rises early in the day
    (*b*) grief at the loss of a loved one
    (*c*) defiance of coldhearted lawmakers
    (*d*) sad music played at a funeral

EXERCISES

Putting Events in Sequence

A.   Write the letters of each set of events in the order in which the events happened in Dorothea Dix's life. For example, would you answer #1 by writing *a-b* or *b-a*? If you need help, look back at the story.

1. *a.* Dorothea goes to live with her grandmother.
   b. Dorothea becomes a schoolteacher.

2. *a.* She becomes very sick with tuberculosis.
   b. She gathers facts about the mentally ill all over Massachusetts.

3. *a.* She is helped by a lawmaker in North Carolina.
   b. She travels all over the West to study the treatment of the mentally ill.

4. *a.* She asks the national government in Washington, D.C., to build hospitals for the mentally ill.
   b. President Franklin Pierce rejects Dorothea's plan.

5. *a.* She lives on the top floor of the state mental hospital in New Jersey.
   b. During the Civil War, she serves as head of army nurses.

Making Inferences

B.   Use what you have learned about Dorothea Lynde Dix to infer, or figure out, the correct choice.

1. It seems reasonable to infer that Dorothea's father, Joseph Dix, may have been:
   (*a*) sick with tuberculosis
   (*b*) a brilliant preacher
   (*c*) disappointed in his lazy daughter
   (*d*) mentally ill

2. Of the following persons, the one whom Dorothea would probably choose as a model to be like is:
(*a*) her father   (*b*) Grandmother Dix
(*c*) Dr. Channing   (*d*) James Dobbin

3. The Massachusetts lawmakers were finally forced to vote money for a hospital by the:
(*a*) facts in Dorothea's report
(*b*) demands of the people of Massachusetts
(*c*) insistence of the governor
(*d*) pleas of the mentally ill

4. You can infer that President Franklin Pierce believed in:
(*a*) national health care
(*b*) states' rights
(*c*) strong national government
(*d*) less power for the states

Understanding Cause and Effect

C.   Write the letter of the best choice.

1. Dorothea's concern for the mentally ill may have come from:
(*a*) the advice of her grandmother
(*b*) her experience as a schoolteacher
(*c*) her pity for her father
(*d*) her own illness

2. As a result of her illness, Dorothea:
(*a*) wrote children's books
(*b*) gave up teaching
(*c*) never married
(*d*) moved to the warmer climate of North Carolina

3. The DIRECT cause of Dorothea's research into the treatment of the insane in Massachusetts was:
(*a*) her grandmother's death
(*b*) her father's mental condition
(*c*) newspaper reports in the state
(*d*) her experience in the jail near Boston

4. As a result of Dorothea's offer to help in the Civil War, she was:
  (*a*) wounded in action
  (*b*) put in charge of the army's nursing program
  (*c*) given a medal by President Lincoln
  (*d*) sent abroad to study hospitals for the insane

Separating Fact from Opinion

D. Tell which is a *fact* and which is an *opinion*.

1. In 1841, Dorothea visited the insane in a jail near Boston.

2. The jailer should not have let her go into that dark and cold place.

3. Dr. William Ellery Channing was obviously a good man.

4. Dorothea visited 500 insane persons in New Jersey.

Choosing the Best Title

E. Write the number of the best title for the story of Dorothea Dix.

1. Wartime Nurse

2. A Pioneer of Prison Reform

3. Angel of Mercy for the Mentally Ill

4. Crusader for Change

Speaking, Listening, and Writing

F. Listen while two or more of your classmates discuss one of the following topics. Be prepared to tell which ideas you most agree with, and why. (*Note*: It may help you to take notes while you listen.)

1. Why do you think people once treated the mentally ill so harshly?

2. If Dorothea Dix were alive today, how could she help people? What problem or problems would you advise her to work on?

G.   Write a paragraph or more about one of the following topics.

1. What did Dorothea mean when she once said, "I had no childhood."

2. What did Dorothea do to persuade state lawmakers to vote money for hospitals for the mentally ill?

3. Pretend that you are Dorothea Dix. Write a short newspaper editorial telling what you think she would do about the problems of homeless people in America today.

A world-famous writer creates laughter out of sorrow.

16. Mark Twain

Part I

1   **Samuel Langhorne Clemens** was born in 1835 in the small town of Florida, Missouri. When he was four, his family moved 30 miles away to Hannibal. This quiet country town lay on the very edge of the Mississippi River. Both the town and the river were home for Sam for the next 14 years of his life.

2   With other boys, he played cowboys and Indians, pirates, and robbers. He roamed through the woods and fields around the town. In the winter, he ice-skated. In warm weather, he swam and fished in the river.

3   Sam learned to love the river. There was always something to see. In the spring, large rafts made of logs floated downstream. Canoes, sailboats, and barges that were like great floating trucks moved up and down the river. From time to time, somebody would shout, "Steamboat coming!" At once, the whole town of Hannibal would wake up.

4   Of all the sights on the Mississippi River, the most exciting were the steamboats. They carried passengers and cargo up and down the hundreds of miles of river. Huge round paddlewheels drove them. Black smoke poured from their two smokestacks. From tall poles on the decks, flags waved. As the steamboats neared Hannibal, they blew horns and rang bells.

5   To young Sam Clemens and his friends, a steamboat

seemed like a floating palace. The most important person on the steamboat was the pilot, who steered and gave the orders. He was like the king of the palace. Sam used to dream that someday he would become a steamboat pilot.

6   The Clemens family often returned to Florida, Missouri, to visit Sam's aunt and uncle. They owned a small farm there. Some of Sam's happiest memories were of those long visits on the farm.

7   Other memories of his childhood were less happy ones. In those days before the Civil War, slavery was part of daily life in Missouri. Many years later, Sam wrote: "I vividly remember seeing a dozen black men and women chained to one another, once, and lying in a group on the pavement, awaiting shipment to the Southern slave market. Those were the saddest faces I have ever seen."

8   Violence and death were never far away. One day, Sam saw a harmless drunk shot down in a Hannibal street. Somebody laid a huge Bible on the man's chest. As Sam watched with horror, the dying man struggled to breathe under the crushing weight of the heavy book.

9   Coming home one evening, Sam passed the town jail. In it was a drunken old man, who had been locked up for the night.

10   "Hey, young fellow!" the old man said. "I got me a pipe but no matches. Can you give me some?" Feeling sorry for the man, Sam gave him a few matches.

11   Later that night, the sound of the town fire alarm woke Sam up. Along with everybody else, he ran to see the fire. It was the jail. The old man must have set it on fire by accident. The flames were so high and the fire so hot that nobody could go near the building. Sam could hear the old man, locked inside, screaming as he burned to death.

12   Sam believed that he was to blame for the death of the old man. After all, hadn't he given him the matches? For a long time afterward, the young boy felt like a criminal. The fact that his father was the town judge only made him feel worse. His dreams were haunted with fears of being found out and punished.

13   Death also struck his own family. Of his four brothers and sisters, two died while Sam was still a young child. In 1847, when he was 11 years old, his father also died suddenly.

14   Judge Clemens had been a stern, cold man. Sam had always been afraid of him. His death greatly shocked his young son. For several nights after the funeral, Sam had terrible nightmares, and even walked in his sleep.

15   The death of his father marked the end of Sam's childhood. His years in Hannibal had been filled with fun and boyish adventures. But his boyhood also had a dark side that he would always remember.

Finding Details

1. Sights and sounds on the Mississippi River are described in paragraphs:
   (a) 1 and 2   (b) 3 and 4   (c) 7 and 8   (d) 14 and 15

2. Give the number of the paragraph in which you learn:
  a. how long Sam Clemens lived in Hannibal, Missouri
  b. what Sam wanted to be when he grew up
  c. who probably set the town jail on fire
  d when Sam's father died

Part II

16   **After his father's death,** Sam quit school and went to work. He was 11 years old. For two years, he served as a printer's apprentice. (An apprentice is taught a trade while working at it.) Sam learned how to set type for newspapers and other printed materials. His first job, after being an apprentice, was on his older brother Orion's newspaper in Hannibal.

17   As a printer, Sam could find work almost anywhere. When he was 17, he left Hannibal and traveled for 10 years from one printing shop to another all over the East. He was making a living, and he was seeing some of the country beyond Hannibal. From time to time, he also wrote short humorous pieces for newspapers and magazines. Yet he wanted something more for himself.

18   Sam decided to try to strike it rich in South America. In 1857, he set off by steamboat down the Mississippi River to New Orleans. On the way down the river, he became friends with the steamboat pilot, Horace Bixby. Here was one of the best pilots on the river. With great care and interest, Sam watched Horace Bixby at work.

19   Sam didn't go to South America after all. Instead, he asked Horace Bixby to teach him to be a pilot. The older man agreed to train him in return for the first $500 he would earn as a pilot.

20   For three years, Sam piloted steamboats up and down the thousand and more miles of the Mississippi

River. He learned to know and love every mile of the wide, winding river. As he stood behind the big steering wheel in the pilot house, he was never happier. He felt that his boyhood dream had come true.

21   Of all the sights and sounds on the river, Sam never forgot the loud calls of the leadsman. This man's job was to tell if the water was at least two fathoms (12 feet) deep—safe water for a steamboat. He did this by lowering a chunk of lead at the end of a rope marked off in fathoms down to the bed of the river.

22   "Mark one!" the leadsman would sing out. This meant the water was only one fathom (six feet) deep.

23   Sam steered the big steamboat slowly and carefully through the shallow water. He was guided by the calls of the leadsman. The pilot could relax only when the water was two (or "twain") fathoms deep. Then he heard the leadsman sing out, "Mark twain! Safe water!"

24   In 1861, the Civil War brought steamboating on the Mississippi River to an end. Sam had to give up his work as a river pilot. It was time for him to move on.

25   He headed west with his brother Orion. For several years, he prospected for silver and gold in Nevada and California. During this time, he also worked as a newspaper reporter. In addition to reporting the news, he wrote humorous stories and articles. He began to sign these humorous writings with the pen name "Mark Twain." Before long, Sam Clemens was better known as Mark Twain.

26   In 1866, Mark Twain visited Hawaii. When he returned to San Francisco, California, he gave a lecture, or public talk, there about his travels. From that time on, Mark Twain was not only a writer, but also a very popular humorous lecturer. In later years, he earned as much as $1500 for one lecture. Speaking in public also helped prepare him for his best writing. Mark Twain always wrote his stories with the sound of a living voice in his mind.

Writing Details

3. In this part of the story, you learn about different kinds of work Sam did. Mention four of them.

4. Using complete and correct sentences, write in your own words where Sam got the pen name Mark Twain.

Part III

27   **In 1867, Mark Twain** was still trying to make a living as a writer. Although he had written some short humorous pieces, he had not yet written a book. In that year, he took a steamboat trip to Europe, hoping to write a book about his trip.

28   On the steamboat, Mark shared a cabin with a young man. One day, he saw a small picture of the young man's sister.

29   "What a beautiful girl!" Mark said. Then he added, "I'm going to marry her someday."

30   The young woman in the picture was Olivia Langdon, the daughter of a rich businessman from Elmira, New York. When Mark returned to New York, he met Olivia. To him, she seemed even more beautiful than her picture. As he visited the Langdon family, he grew even more certain that Olivia Langdon would become his wife.

31   Olivia's father was not so sure. Who was this young man from the West who wanted to marry his daughter? Mr. Langdon told Mark that he must ask people he knew to write letters about him. So Mark wrote to his old pals in Nevada and California.

32   One day, Mr. Langdon called Mark into his office. He had heard from the young man's friends. All of them

had decided to play a joke on Mark by saying terrible things about him.

33   "I must tell you," Mr. Langdon said in a serious voice, "that all six of your friends had nothing good to say about you. They warned me that you are lazy. They said that you smoke and curse. Two of them even thought that you would end up drinking yourself to death."

34   For the first time in his life, Mark stood speechless. All his dreams of marrying Olivia seemed crushed.

35   "Well," Mr. Langdon said at last, "if your own friends won't speak up for you, I guess I will have to do it myself. I like you, Mr. Clemens, and I trust you to be good to my daughter. I will let her marry you." In February 1870, Olivia Langdon married Samuel Clemens.

36   Mark Twain wrote his first important book, called *The Innocents Abroad*, in 1869. It was a very funny book in which he told about his trip to Europe. In *Roughing It*, he told the true story of his years out West. In *Life on the Mississippi*, he wrote about his training and work as a steamboat pilot. With their fresh, lively humor, these books sold well. His writing and his lecturing were making Mark rich.

37   In 1873, he bought a large piece of land in Hartford, Connecticut. For 20 years, Mark and his wife lived in the fine house he built there. They had three daughters: Susy, Clara, and Jean. A cook, a butler, a gardener, and other servants worked in the big house. In addition, the house was always full of guests.

38   These were busy and happy years for Mark, but they were also a strain on him. To keep up his rich way of life, he had to make more and more money. Besides lecturing and writing, he poured hundreds of thousands of dollars into schemes for making even more money. As a famous author, he had little peace and quiet. Friends, visitors, and newspaper reporters took up much of his time.

39   Often he remembered the long, lazy, carefree times of his childhood. In his two greatest novels, he wrote about life in a small town in Missouri. For Mark, these books were a way of escaping from the strains and worries of life in Hartford. Writing them was like going back to his hometown of Hannibal.

40   The first of his two great novels about boyhood is *The Adventures of Tom Sawyer* (1876). In this book, Mark wrote with love and humor about Tom and his young friends Joe Harper and Huckleberry (Huck) Finn. *The Adventures of Huckleberry Finn* (1885) continues the story

of Tom Sawyer and Huck Finn. This time, however, it is Huck's own story. In fact, the novel is written as if Huck were speaking and telling the story.

41   *Huckleberry Finn* is the first important novel written entirely in the everyday speech of ordinary people. It is a very funny book. At the same time, it is a very serious book. How can this be?

42   The novel tells the humorous story of Huck Finn and Tom Sawyer's adventures. It also tells how Huck helps Jim, a black man, escape from slavery. Together, Huck and Jim float down the Mississippi River on a raft, passing through many troubles and dangers. Some of the worst troubles, though, are in Huck's own head.

43   Although Huck has been raised to believe that slavery is right, he has learned to love Jim as a true and trusted friend. Huck's head tells him to turn Jim in. But Huck's heart tells him to help Jim escape.

44   As he wrote the story, Mark remembered the beauty and joy of his childhood and also its violence and hate and fears. He wrote all of it into his story. Most people believe that *Huckleberry Finn* is Mark Twain's finest novel. Some people think that it is the greatest American novel.

Finding the Main Idea

5. The main idea of paragraph 31 is:
    (*a*) Mark's marriage to Olivia
    (*b*) the joke Mark's friends played on him
    (*c*) Mr. Langdon's request for letters of reference
    (*d*) life in the Langdon family

6. The main idea of paragraphs 37–38 concerns Mark's
    (*a*) life in Hartford
    (*b*) books about his earlier life
    (*c*) family
    (*d*) schemes for getting rich

Part IV

45   **From his books and his lectures,** Mark Twain earned as much as $100,000 a year, a great deal of money a century ago. Unfortunately, he spent money even faster than he made it. He spent about $200,000 on a new machine for setting type. When the machine couldn't be made to work, he lost all the money he had invested in it.

46   In the early 1890s, his good luck ran out. He found himself deeply in debt. His own money was all gone, and, even worse, he had also lost his wife's money. To pay back all the money he owed, Mark went on a lecture tour around the world. Wherever he went, he made people laugh. Only those who were close to him knew how worried and tired he really was.

47   While Mark and his wife were in Europe, their daughter Susy died in America at the age of 23. Eight years later, Mark's beloved wife Olivia died. Then, five years after that, his daughter Jean also died. She was only 30 years old.

48   Mark Twain was filled with sorrow. In public, however, he was still America's great humorist. Somehow, he had always understood how this could be. Years earlier, he had written, "The secret source of humor itself is not joy but sorrow."

49   These later years of Mark's life were not all filled with sorrow. There were joys, too. People all over the world read and enjoyed his books. Wherever he went, he was treated like a king. Everyone loved and admired Mark Twain.

50   Three universities honored him with degrees. He was proudest of his degree from Oxford University in England. What an honor for a man who had left school at the age of 11!

51   As an old man, Mark enjoyed the company of young girls. Perhaps they reminded him of the daughters he had lost. He became a good friend of Helen Keller, a blind and deaf young girl. With great effort, she had learned to read and write and understand speech—all with her fingers. Mark liked to tell Helen stories while she sat and "listened" with her fingers on his lips.

52   The last important book that Mark wrote was the story of his life. In his old age, his mind went back to the early years of his youth in Hannibal, Missouri. He remembered it all as if it were only yesterday. This book contains some of his most humorous and most beautiful writing.

53   Mark Twain died in 1910 at the age of 74. His body was taken to a church in New York City. Thousands of people lined up in the rain to say good-bye to the man whose books had brought laughter to the whole world.

Working with Words

7. When young Sam *roamed* (paragraph 2) through the woods and fields, he most probably:
   (*a*) became lost   (*b*) raced
   (*c*) wandered about   (*d*) climbed trees

8. Something *vividly* (paragraph 7) remembered is remembered:
   (*a*) sadly   (*b*) clearly   (*c*) with difficulty   (*d*) happily

9. A *pen name* (paragraph 25) is one used by a:
   (*a*) criminal
   (*b*) steamboat pilot
   (*c*) gold and silver prospector
   (*d*) writer

10. In paragraph 38, *strain* most nearly means a:
    (*a*) wrenched or pulled muscle
    (*b*) kind or sort of thing
    (*c*) heavy burden
    (*d*) source of great pleasure

EXERCISES

Putting Events in Sequence

A.   Write the letters of each set of events in the order in which the events happened in Sam Clemens' (Mark Twain's) life. For example, would you answer #1 by writing *a-b* or *b-a*? If you need help, look back at the story.

1. *a.* Sam travels all over the East, working as a printer.
 b. His father, Judge Clemens, dies.

2. *a.* The Civil War begins.
 b. Sam becomes a steamboat pilot on the Mississippi River.

3. *a.* Sam and Olivia Langdon marry.
 b. He hunts for gold and silver out West.

4. *a.* He writes *The Adventures of Tom Sawyer.*
 b. He writes *The Adventures of Huckleberry Finn.*

5. *a.* His wife and two of his daughters die.
 b. He writes the story of his life.

Making Inferences

B.   Use what you have read about Mark Twain to infer, or figure out, the correct choice.

1. Mark Twain was born:
 (*a*) before the American Revolution
 (*b*) before the Civil War
 (*c*) during the Civil War
 (*d*) after the Civil War

2. The materials in Mark's books came chiefly from:
 (*a*) his reading   (*b*) his own life
 (*c*) history   (*d*) research in libraries

3. From the story of Mark's adult life, you can safely infer that he was:
   (*a*) an unsuccessful author
   (*b*) a cold, stern father
   (*c*) a lazy man
   (*d*) a poor businessman

4. As you know, nonfiction tells about things that really happened, while fiction, such as novels or short stories, tells a make-believe story. With this distinction in mind, you could infer that Mark Twain wrote:
   (*a*) nonfiction only
   (*b*) fiction only
   (*c*) both nonfiction and fiction
   (*d*) neither nonfiction nor fiction

Understanding Cause and Effect

   C.   Write the letter of the correct choice.

1. Because of the Civil War, Mark had to:
   (*a*) give up his career as a steamboat pilot
   (*b*) become a printer
   (*c*) serve as a war correspondent, or reporter
   (*d*) stop prospecting for gold and silver

2. As a result of the letters Mr. Langdon received from Mark's old pals, Olivia's father:
   (*a*) refused to let Mark marry Olivia
   (*b*) allowed Mark to marry Olivia anyway
   (*c*) told Mark to ask for more letters
   (*d*) wrote letters to each of the old pals

3. Huck Finn is in great conflict because:
   (*a*) he believes slavery is wrong, but he wants to return Jim, an escaped slave, to slavery
   (*b*) he believes slavery is right, but he wants to help Jim escape from slavery
   (*c*) he disapproves of his friend Tom Sawyer's adventures
   (*d*) he knows that there are many troubles and dangers on the Mississippi River

4. Mark believed that humor resulted from:
(*a*) life's comedy (*b*) laughter (*c*) joy (*d*) sorrow

Separating Fact from Opinion

D. Tell which is a *fact* and which is an *opinion*.

1. Mark's boyhood was spent near the Mississippi River.

2. The Mississippi is a beautiful river.

3. *The Adventures of Huckleberry Finn* is the greatest American novel.

4. When Mark Twain died in 1910 at the age of 74, he was the world's favorite author.

Choosing the Best Title

E. Write the number of the best title for the story of Mark Twain.

1. The Happy Steamboat Pilot

2. A Fighter Against Slavery

3. A Writer of Tears, Fears, and Laughter

4. Life on the Mississippi

Speaking, Listening, and Writing

F. Be prepared to talk briefly about one of the following topics.

1. Do you know someone who is very humorous? How is he or she funny? (You may wish to make up a name for the real person you choose to tell about.)

2. How well do you remember your own childhood? Tell one or two of your earliest memories so that they seem real to your listeners.

G.   Write a paragraph or more about one of the following topics.

1. What were some of the good things in Sam Clemens' childhood?

2. What were some of the bad or frightening things in his childhood?

3. What was the joke Mark Twain's friends played on him when he wanted to marry Olivia Langdon? How did the joke turn out? You might try writing about the joke in a dialog (as in a play) between Mark Twain and Mr. Langdon.

One of America's greatest black leaders lives and dies for his dream.

17. Martin Luther King, Jr.

Part I

1   **Martin Luther King, Jr.,** was born in 1929 in Atlanta, Georgia. His parents and his grandfather were teachers, ministers, and leaders in the black community. Thus, the shaping forces in Martin's family background were education, the church, and a deep concern for the welfare of black people.

2   Martin's childhood was comfortable and secure. With his older sister and younger brother, he grew up in a warm and loving middle-class family. Books, daily prayers, and church matters were an important part of his family life.

3   In the larger world outside his family, however, Martin couldn't help learning how badly black people were treated. He saw how they had to use the rear door and seats on a bus. He saw signs in stores that read "For Whites Only."

4   Martin grew up to be a gifted boy. He read widely, sang beautifully, and spoke unusually well. His mother used to take him to nearby churches, where he sang for the members. In high school, he spoke well enough to take part in a statewide public-speaking contest. In later years, these gifts served him well.

5   Martin was only 15 years old when he entered More-house College in Atlanta. His father had also gone to this all-black college. At that time, schools in the South were strictly segregated, which meant that black students and white students went to separate schools.

6   At Morehouse College, two important things happened to Martin. He decided to become a minister, like his father and his grandfather, and he read the essay "Civil Disobedience" by Henry David Thoreau, a 19th-century American writer. This essay, written a hundred years earlier, helped point the way to Martin's lifework.

7   Years before the Civil War, Thoreau spoke out against slavery. Rather than support a government that allowed slavery in America, he refused to pay his taxes. For this, he was put into jail.

8   In the essay "Civil Disobedience," Thoreau wrote that people should not obey a bad law. Doing what is right, he argued, is more important than obeying an unjust law. He believed that it is better to go to jail peacefully, as he did, than to obey a harmful law.

9   Reading this essay, Martin's heart was stirred. He saw that civil disobedience could be used against the laws that treated black people unfairly. Here was a peaceful way for a man of God to fight injustice.

10   After graduating from college in 1948, Martin went to Crozer Theological Seminary in Pennsylvania. The most important thing that happened to him there was his discovery of Mahatma Gandhi. Martin read all the books that he could find about this great leader of India. Gandhi helped free his country from British rule. From 1920 to 1947, he led the people of India in nonviolent resistance to unjust British laws.

11   The British often put Gandhi into jail for his acts of civil disobedience. (Many years earlier, Gandhi had also read Thoreau's essay "Civil Disobedience.") But courage and nonviolence won in the end. In 1947, Great Britain gave India its freedom. Like Thoreau, Gandhi greatly influenced Martin.

12   Of course, nobody had a greater influence on his life and work than Jesus Christ. "Love your enemies," Jesus taught. "Bless them that curse you, do good to them that hurt you." A person who followed this teaching had to lead a life of nonviolence.

13   In 1951, Martin entered Boston University in Massachusetts. While he was studying there, he met Coretta Scott. A talented singer, she was attending the nearby New England Conservatory of Music. Two years later, they were married.

14   With a degree from Boston University, Martin could have his choice of jobs. He could teach in a college, or he could become the minister of a church either in the North or in the South. He decided to accept a position as pastor of the Dexter Avenue Baptist Church in Montgomery, Alabama.

Finding Details

1. Three important influences on Martin Luther King, Jr., are discussed in paragraphs:
   (*a*) 1–5   (*b*) 6–9   (*c*) 10–12   (*d*) 6–12

2. Martin's first job is mentioned in paragraph:
   (*a*) 4   (*b*) 10   (*c*) 13   (*d*) 14

Part II

15   **When Martin and Coretta King** settled in Montgomery, Alabama, a spirit of unrest was growing among black people. They were no longer willing to remain second-class citizens. Black Americans had served bravely during World War II. They had fought for democracy in other parts of the world. "Why," they asked, "should we still be denied our democratic rights at home?"

16   Segregation—the separate and unequal treatment of blacks by whites—was the custom in the North. In the South, it was the law. In May 1954, the United States Supreme Court outlawed segregation in public schools. But segregation continued in all other public places, including the buses of Montgomery, Alabama.

17   At this time, black passengers were not allowed to sit in the front, which was reserved for white passengers. When the front of the bus was full and more white passengers came on board, the black passengers had to give up their seats and move even farther to the rear. If the rest of the bus was full, they had to ride standing.

18   On Thursday, December 1, 1955, something important happened. On that day, Mrs. Rosa Parks, a middle-aged black woman, refused to give up her seat to a white man. This one small event helped change the course of American history. It also marked the beginning of Martin's lifework.

19   When Mrs. Parks refused to move, the bus driver called the police. Two police officers arrested her and took her to jail. News of Mrs. Parks' arrest spread quickly among the black leaders of Montgomery.

20   The black leaders began to make plans. Now, they felt, was the time to act. They decided to protest Mrs. Parks' arrest by a one-day boycott of the buses. Every black person in Montgomery was urged to stay off the buses for one full day.

21   The boycott was a complete success. About 70 percent of the bus company's customers were black. All day long, the yellow buses drove up and down the streets of Montgomery almost empty.

22   Later that day, the black leaders of Montgomery decided to keep up the boycott until the company promised black riders better treatment. In time, the boycott grew into a movement to end segregation on the buses. To run the boycott, the leaders set up the Montgomery Improvement Association. As president, they elected Martin Luther King, Jr. He gave his people the kind of

leadership they needed. He kept the boycott nonviolent, and he kept it alive.

23   As leader of the movement, Martin was in constant danger. He had more than himself to worry about, though. At home were Coretta and their new baby girl. Day and night, voices made ugly threats on their telephone. One evening, their house was bombed. The blast tore open the front porch and smashed the living room windows. Fortunately, the family was not hurt.

24   Over a thousand angry black people quickly gathered in front of the King house. They were armed with sticks, rocks, knives, and guns. Police, fire fighters, and even the mayor of Montgomery were there. At any minute, a bloody riot seemed certain to explode.

25   Martin stepped onto his blasted front porch. He stood there for a minute, studying the crowd. Then he raised his hand. The crowd grew silent.

26   "My wife and my baby are all right," he said. "I want you to go home and put down your weapons. We must meet violence with nonviolence. Remember the words of Jesus: 'He who lives by the sword will perish by the sword.' This is what we must live by. We must meet hate with love."

27   The crowd was deeply moved. Here was a man whose home had just been bombed, whose wife and baby had almost been killed. Yet he spoke of nonviolence and love. With cries of "Amen!" and "God bless you, Reverend," the crowd broke up and went home.

28   The next day, newspapers all over America carried the story of what had happened in Montgomery. Hate and violence had been answered with love and peace. By his own brave example, Martin had shown his people the way of nonviolence.

29   The boycott of the bus company lasted an entire year. Although it began in the streets, it was finally settled in the courts. Late in 1956, the United States Supreme Court ruled that bus segregation in Alabama would have to end.

30   On the morning of December 21, while a crowd of newspaper and television reporters watched, a bus stopped in front of the King house. This was the moment everybody had been waiting for. Martin Luther King, Mrs. Rosa Parks, and other black leaders and white leaders of the bus boycott entered at the front door of the bus. Together they sat down in the front seats. The bus driver smiled, welcomed them aboard, closed the door, and drove on. How easy it all seemed!

31   But some white people of Montgomery were afraid to see the old ways change. A few days after segregation had ended on the buses, violence broke out in Montgomery. White men shot at the buses and beat up black bus riders. They blew up the home and church of Reverend Ralph Abernathy, a close friend of Martin. They also bombed three other Baptist churches.

32   These acts of violence left Martin terribly upset. At a mass meeting, he prayed, "Lord, I hope no one will have to die as a result of our struggle for freedom in Montgomery. Certainly I don't want to die. But if anyone has to die, let it be me."

33   After a while, the violence stopped. Property had been damaged and black people had been hurt. In all that time, however, no one had been killed. Most important of all, Martin had taught his people a new way to win their rights.

Writing Details

3. Complete the following sentences by supplying the missing information.
   a. In 1955, black residents of _____ boycotted the buses.
   b. They chose _____ to lead the boycott.
   c. When Martin's house was bombed, he urged his black neighbors not to resort to _____.
   d. Bus segregation was ruled illegal in 1956 by the _____.

4. Paragraph 33 states that "Martin had taught his people a new way to win their rights." In a complete and correct sentence or two, tell what that new way was.

<u>Part III</u>

34   **So far, Martin Luther King's** efforts had been limited to Montgomery, Alabama. Now he was ready to broaden his work for civil rights throughout the South. With his friend Ralph Abernathy and other black ministers, he helped form the Southern Christian Leadership Conference (SCLC). Reverend King was elected president of the new organization. The SCLC raised money and worked to 'end racial segregation. It also helped black Southerners register and vote in elections.

35   Martin decided to give more time to the civil-rights movement. In 1960, he moved to Atlanta, Georgia, where the SCLC offices were. He also joined his father there as co-pastor of the Ebenezer Baptist Church.

36   In the early 1960s, the use of nonviolent resistance to segregation spread throughout the South. Black students and adults staged sit-ins at segregated lunch counters, restaurants, movie theaters, and other public places. There were peaceful marches in all the major cities of the South.

37   Martin led many of these sit-ins and marches. His growing family saw little of him during that time. Again and again, he was put into Southern jails. He also traveled all over the country, making speeches to raise money. To audiences, he would quote the words of an old black slave: "We ain't what we ought to be and we ain't what we want to be. But thank God we ain't what we was."

38   After the sit-ins came the freedom rides. From all over the country, white students joined black students on the segregated interstate buses. As these buses that traveled from one state to another rolled into Southern cities, angry white mobs attacked the freedom riders. But slowly, bit by bit, the walls of segregation were crumbling.

39   Martin led large marches against segregation in Albany, Georgia, and in Birmingham, Alabama. In each city, he was arrested and put into jail. The Birmingham police attacked the peaceful marchers with fire hoses, clubs, tear gas, and fierce dogs. But Martin and the marchers could not be stopped. They came back, marching and singing the song of the civil-rights movement—"We Shall Overcome."

40   On August 28, 1963, came the biggest march of all. More than a million people marched on Washington, D.C. They came from all parts of the country, black and white, young and old. They were there to urge the United States Congress to vote for a civil-rights bill that would end segregation in all public places.

41   Standing in front of the Lincoln Memorial, Martin spoke to the vast crowd of his hope and faith in America. Radio and television carried these words all over America.

42   "I have a dream," he said, "that one day this nation will rise up and live out the true meaning of its creed: 'We hold these truths to be self-evident, that all men are created equal.'"

43   "I have a dream," he went on, "that my four little children will one day live in a nation where they will not be judged by the color of their skin but by the content of their character."

44   His strong, musical voice rose as he spoke of the day when all Americans would be able "to join hands and sing in the words of that old Negro spiritual, 'Free at last! Free at last! Thank God almighty, we're free at last!'"

45   It was his greatest speech. The people of America would not forget those ringing words. But no one knew better than Martin Luther King how long and bitter a fight for freedom still remained.

Finding the Main Idea

5. A main idea of this part of the story is the fight against:
   (*a*) religious prejudice   (*b*) poverty
   (*c*) racial segregation   (*d*) election fraud

6. A second main idea of this part of the story is:
   (*a*) the formation of the Southern Christian Leadership Conference (SCLC)
   (*b*) the spread of the civil rights movement throughout the South
   (*c*) the march on Washington, D.C., in 1963
   (*d*) Martin's great "I have a dream" speech

Part IV

46   **Back in Birmingham,** the forces of fear and hate set to work. The homes of black civil-rights leaders were bombed. A black man was shot to death. One Sunday morning, a bomb exploded at the Sixteenth Street Baptist Church. Twenty-one black men and women were badly hurt, and four young girls were killed.

47   In spite of these brutal acts of violence, Martin urged his people to remain firm. "We must not become bitter," he said at the funeral services for the four young girls. "We must not lose faith in our white brothers."

48   In 1964, Martin received the greatest honor of his life. He was awarded the Nobel Peace Prize. Each year, this prize is given to the person, anywhere in the world, who has done the most for the cause of peace.

49   At the age of 35, Reverend King was the youngest person ever to be awarded this honor. With his proud family and friends, he traveled to Norway to receive the Nobel medal and $54,000. He gave all the prize money to groups working for civil rights for black Americans.

50   Returning to America, Martin plunged back into his work. He led a movement in Selma, Alabama, to register black voters and end segregation in the city's hotels, eating places, and theaters. His work also began to take him far beyond the borders of the South.

51   He set up Organization Breadbasket in the northern city of Chicago, Illinois. Its purpose was to find jobs for black workers. He also began to speak out against America's role in the war in Vietnam.

52   These new directions in his work made new enemies for him. Many Americans, both black and white, were angered by his criticism of the Vietnam War. They feared that, without meaning to, he was helping the Communists. He should stick to civil rights, they felt, and not talk about politics.

Martin Luther King, Jr., is in front, third from left.

53   To Martin, however, civil rights and politics could not be separated. President Lyndon Johnson hoped to make a "Great Society" for all Americans. But Martin pointed out that, for poor Americans, the promised Great Society was being set aside in favor of the war.

54   "The Great Society," he said in a speech early in 1967, "has been shot down on the battlefields of Vietnam."

55   Some young black leaders no longer accepted nonviolence as a way to win equality. Raising the cry of "black power," they rejected Martin's way of love and peace. In the big cities, riots broke out. Black neighborhoods burned in New York, Newark, and Detroit. The worst riot was in the Watts section of Los Angeles. The Kerner Commission, set up in 1968 to report on the riots, concluded that "our nation is moving toward two societies, one black, one white—separate and unequal."

56   Early in 1968, Martin planned a Poor People's March on Washington. This march was to be different from the one in 1963. Five years ago, his concern had been for *civil* rights—the right to vote and the end of segregation. Now his concern was for *human* rights—decent housing and jobs for black Americans

57   Before the Poor People's March took place, however, Martin went to Memphis, Tennessee. Black workers in that city were on strike for higher wages and better working conditions. The world-famous black leader visited Memphis to help win support for the strike. On April 4, as Reverend King stood on the balcony of his motel room, he was shot to death.

58   The night before his death, Martin spoke to a large audience in Memphis:

> I don't know what will happen now. But it really doesn't matter with me now. Like anybody, I would like to live a long life. But I'm not concerned about that now. I just want to do God's will. And He's allowed me to go up to the mountain. And I've looked over, and I've seen the promised land. I may not get there with you. But I want you to know tonight that we as a people will get to the promised land.

Working with Words

7. *Resistance* (paragraph 10) to an unjust law is a kind of:
   (*a*) opposition   (*b*) surrender   (*c*) obedience   (*d*) neglect

8. People who are *denied* (paragraph 15) their rights can best be described as:
   (*a*) fortunate   (*b*) deprived   (*c*) privileged   (*d*) determined

9. If *interstate* (paragraph 38) means "between states," match each word at the left with its correct meaning at the right.
   a. international   (1) between or among colleges
   b. interpersonal   (2) between nations
   c. intercollegiate   (3) depending on each other
   d. interdependent   (4) between two or more people

10. When young black leaders *rejected* (paragraph 55) nonviolence, they:

    (*a*) supported peaceful resistance

    (*b*) became followers of Martin Luther King, Jr.

    (*c*) took up political activity

    (*d*) turned to violent action

EXERCISES

Putting Events in Sequence

A. Write the letters of each set of events in the order in which the events happened in the life of Martin Luther King, Jr. For example, would you answer #1 by writing *a-b* or *b-a*? If you need help, look back at the story.

1. *a.* Martin reads Thoreau's essay "Civil Disobedience."

    b. He becomes pastor of a church in Montgomery, Alabama.

2. *a.* The black people of Montgomery boycott the city buses.

    b. Mrs. Rosa Parks is arrested in Montgomery.

3. *a.* Martin's house is bombed.

    b. The Supreme Court ends segregation on buses in Montgomery.

4. *a.* Martin is given the Nobel Peace Prize.

    b. He tells a huge crowd in Washington, D.C., "I have a dream."

5. *a.* He helps form the Southern Christian Leadership Conference.

    b. Black people riot in Watts, California.

Making Inferences

B. Use what you have read about Martin Luther King, Jr., to infer, or figure out, the correct choice.

1. As a student, Martin was strongly influenced by his:

    (*a*) mother   (*b*) wife   (*c*) grandfather   (*d*) reading

2. As time passed, the goals of the Montgomery bus boycott:
    (*a*) became narrower   (*b*) became broader
    (*c*) were forgotten   (*d*) were abandoned

3. You can infer that each time Martin was arrested and put into jail, most black people regarded him as:
    (*a*) a victim   (*b*) a hero   (*c*) a martyr   (*d*) all of these

4. Which of the following is a direct statement, NOT an inference?
    (*a*) Martin's deeds and words suggest that he believed religion should help people improve their lives peacefully.
    (*b*) It must have taken courage for Mrs. Rosa Parks to refuse to give up her seat on the bus.
    (*c*) Martin was elected president of the Southern Christian Leadership Conference (SCLC).
    (*d*) Like Gandhi and Jesus, Martin evidently felt that his actions should set an example for others.

Understanding Cause and Effect

    C.   Write the letter of the correct choice.

1. In which order did the following three men influence each other?
    (*a*) Gandhi → King → Thoreau
    (*b*) Gandhi → Thoreau → King
    (*c*) Thoreau → King → Gandhi
    (*d*) Thoreau → Gandhi → King

2. An immediate effect of the arrest of Mrs. Rosa Parks was the:
    (*a*) bus boycott
    (*b*) bombing of Martin's house
    (*c*) Supreme Court ruling
    (*d*) bombing of churches

3. A frequent effect of black people's peaceful resistance to racial segregation was:
    (*a*) Supreme Court rulings
    (*b*) violence by white people
    (*c*) marches on Washington, D.C.
    (*d*) sit-ins and freedom rides

4. The Kerner Commission was established because of:
(*a*) violence by white people
(*b*) sit-ins and freedom rides
(*c*) riots in black neighborhoods of big cities
(*d*) the Vietnam War

Separating Fact from Opinion

D. Tell which is a *fact* and which is an *opinion*.

1. Martin's lifework took place after World War II.

2. Martin was a brave man.

3. Martin's life was often threatened.

4. Martin should have taken more care for his own life.

Choosing the Best Title

E. Write the number of the best title for the story of Martin Luther King, Jr.

1. A Great Black Leader

2. The Nobel Peace Prize

3. The Murder of Martin Luther King, Jr.

4. Civil Disobedience

Speaking, Listening, and Writing

F. Listen while two or more of your classmates debate, or take sides on, one of the following topics. Be prepared to tell which side you think made the better argument—and why. (*Hint:* It may help you if you take notes while you listen.)

1. Explain what "civil disobedience" means. Do you agree with the idea of civil disobedience? Give your reasons.

2. How do you think Martin Luther King, Jr., would feel about the most recent war in which Americans fought? Would you agree or disagree with his opinion? Give your reasons.

G.   Write a paragraph or more about one of the following topics.

1. How did the Montgomery bus boycott begin?

2. When his house in Montgomery was bombed, what did Martin Luther King, Jr., do? Why? Write your answer in the form of a short news article with a headline.

3. Do you think Martin Luther King, Jr., would approve of any war? Explain your answer.

Out of a dark and silent world, a young girl learns to love and serve others.

18. *Anne Sullivan and Helen Keller*

<u>Part I</u>

1   **Miss Anne Sullivan peered** out the window of the railroad train. Even though she was wearing dark glasses, the bright sunlight still hurt her eyes.

2   "That doesn't matter now," she thought. "All that matters is my job. This afternoon, I am starting a new job and a new life."

3   The train stopped at the little Southern town of Tuscumbia, Alabama. The young woman's heart beat faster. Once again, she tried to picture Helen Keller. What would the little girl be like?

4   Anne knew only a few facts about Helen. She was almost seven years old. She was completely blind. She was also completely deaf. Because she could not see or hear, the child had never learned to talk. And now, on March 3, 1887, Anne Sullivan had come to be her teacher.

5   Miss Sullivan knew what it was like to be blind. As a child, she had been ill and gradually lost her eyesight. Only a short time ago, an operation had enabled her to see again. Behind her dark glasses, however, her eyes were still weak. If she used them too much, they hurt her. Everything still looked a bit blurred to Anne.

6   Anne's job was to teach Helen to use language. But how could she teach words and ideas to a child who could not see or hear or speak? Could it be done?

7   In order to teach Helen, Anne had learned the manual, or hand, alphabet. In the hand alphabet, each position of the fingers and hand stands for a letter of the alphabet. Being blind, Helen could not see the hand alphabet. So Anne would have to "spell" each letter of a word into the palm of her hand.

8   Anne had brought a present for her new pupil—a doll. She placed the doll in Helen's arms. Then, using the hand alphabet, she spelled the word *d-o-l-l* into Helen's palm. Helen looked puzzled. Again her teacher's fingers spelled out *d-o-l-l*.

9   Helen liked to copy other people's actions. She was very good at it. In a short while, she was able to make the letters *d-o-l-l* herself. As the days went by, she learned other words, but she learned them as a parrot learns. Like a parrot, she had no idea that these words were names for things. Helen had not yet learned to use language.

10   She had not yet learned something just as important. The child knew no limits. She had no self-control. And no wonder! Although Helen was a strong, healthy, and active little girl, she was locked up in a life of endless silence and darkness. She was like a prisoner in her own body.

11   Often the frustration of not being able to see, hear, or speak grew too great. Then she burst into fits of wild temper. She broke things, or she threw herself down on the floor and screamed.

12   Her loving parents only made matters worse. They felt sorry for her. Mr. and Mrs. Keller could not bear to see their daughter suffer. In almost all things, they let her have her own way.

13   "I saw clearly," Anne wrote about Helen, "that it was useless to try to teach her language or anything else until she learned to obey me."

14   Anne also saw that she could never teach Helen to obey while her parents were around. So the teacher and her pupil went to live for two weeks in a small garden house near the Keller home. There the battle between Anne Sullivan and Helen Keller was fought to the end.

15   At first, Helen lay on the floor and kicked and screamed. She would not let Anne touch her. At bedtime, there was a terrific fight that lasted for two hours. Helen was a strong and stubborn child, but Anne Sullivan was stronger and even more stubborn.

16   In the end, Helen learned to obey. She even sat on Anne's lap and let her kiss her. Back in the Keller home again, Helen seemed like a different child. She was able to sit quietly now, and she did as she was told.

Finding Details

1. Which paragraph tells:
   a. where the story takes place
   b. when the story takes place
   c. what the hand alphabet is
   d. how the battle of wills between Helen and Anne ended

2. In which paragraph do you learn something about Anne Sullivan's past?
   (a) 3   (b) 4   (c) 5   (d) 6

Part II

17   **Learning to obey** was the first big step in Helen's education. On the morning of April 5, 1887, she took the second great step. Anne had just taught her a new word. Into her palm, she had spelled w-a-t-e-r. Then the teacher had an idea. She took Helen by the hand and led her out to the pump house.

18   Anne worked the pump handle up and down. The cold water poured over one of Helen's hands. Into the other hand, her teacher spelled again and again *w-a-t-e-r*, *w-a-t-e-r*, *w-a-t-e-r*.

19   Suddenly, a light seemed to come over Helen's face. She felt the cold, wet water splashing over one hand. And she felt the word *w-a-t-e-r* spelled into her other hand. All at once, she grasped the idea—THINGS HAVE NAMES! For the first time, she understood the secret of language.

20   Helen danced about with excitement. She wanted to know more and more words. She touched the ground, and Anne spelled *g-r-o-u-n-d* for her. She touched the pump and the door. Her teacher spelled their names into her hand. She asked for Anne Sullivan's name and learned another new word—*t-e-a-c-h-e-r*. Before the day was done, Helen had learned 30 new words.

21   As Anne wrote about Helen later that same day, "She has learned that everything has a name, and that the hand alphabet is the key to everything she wants to know."

22   From that day on, Helen was eager to learn, and Anne was even more eager to teach her. The teaching

and learning took place everywhere and at all times. Few pupils ever had a better teacher than Anne Sullivan. She had the good sense to make learning a part of Helen's everyday life. She taught Helen in the garden. She taught her at the dinner table. When they went for walks or climbed a tree together or went swimming, the lessons went on.

23 Into Helen's hand, her teacher spelled out the names of things, colors, shapes, smells, sounds, and even ideas and feelings. Before long, Anne began to teach her reading, writing, arithmetic, and other subjects.

24 Most important of all, Anne always treated her pupil like any normal, healthy child. And she made other people treat her that way, too. She took Helen visiting. She took her to parties and even to a circus. She let Helen touch everything. All the time, Anne's rapidly moving fingers described these things for Helen.

25 Anne also taught her to read using Braille. Books printed in Braille have raised dots, like little bumps, on the pages. A different set of dots stands for each letter of the alphabet. A blind person reads Braille with his or her fingertips.

26 In addition to the hand alphabet and Braille, Helen also learned to "read lips." By placing her fingers lightly upon another person's lips, she was able to understand

almost everything the person said. In time, she became very skillful at "lip reading."

27   Even with all these skills, Helen was not content. She also wanted to learn to speak like everyone else.

28   "Blind girls speak with their mouths," she spelled into her teacher's hand one day. "I can feel it when I touch their mouths and their throats. Why don't you teach me to speak, too?"

29   "Even though they can't see, they can hear the sounds of speech," Anne spelled back into her hand. "That makes it possible for them to learn to speak."

30   Helen still was not satisfied. "But don't deaf children ever learn to speak?"

31   "Yes, Helen," her teacher spelled quickly. "Some deaf children learn to speak, but they can see their teachers' mouths."

32   "I have learned to 'see' with my fingers," Helen insisted. "I am sure that I can learn to speak with my mouth as other people do."

33   When she was 10 years old, Helen set to work to learn how to speak. In the spring of 1890, Anne took her to a speech teacher. The teacher gave Helen 11 lessons. After all those years of silence, the work of learning to use her voice was terribly hard, but she did it.

34   Helen's voice never sounded really clear and natural. After all, she could not hear what it sounded like. But the wonder is that she was able to talk at all. She proved that even people who are both deaf and blind can learn to speak.

35   Helen learned more rapidly than children her age who could see and hear. Since she did not have the world of sights and sounds to interest and amuse her, reading and learning served to fill her mind. With Anne's help, she learned to read and write English very well, but she did not stop at English. By the time she was 10, she had also learned to read and write French. A few years later, she learned German, Latin, and Greek, too.

Writing Details

3. In your own words, explain in a sentence or two how Helen discovered the key to the way language works.

4. Tell the three different ways in which Helen was able to read.

Part III

36   **Newspapers and magazines** began printing stories about Helen Keller. People all over America wanted to know more about her. Before long, her fame spread to Europe and other parts of the world. The amazing story of the blind and deaf little girl and her teacher was heard everywhere.

37   Something about Helen pleased and delighted all who met her. Perhaps it was her lively interest in everyone and everything around her. Perhaps it was her pure joy in living. People wondered how a young girl living in silence and darkness could be so cheerful and happy.

38   Many famous men and women were glad to be her friends. The great American writer Mark Twain enjoyed her company. With Helen seated beside him, he would tell funny stories while she "listened" with her fingers on his lips.

39   Another friend was Doctor Alexander Graham Bell. Most people think of him only as the inventor of the telephone. But his lifelong interest was in working with deaf people. Doctor Bell, who was deeply interested in Helen's education, saw much of the young girl in the 1890s.

40   By the time she was 16, Helen had made up her mind to go to college. She wanted to go to Radcliffe, the college for women at Harvard University. But there was a problem.

41   In 1896, her father died. Although he left some money, it was not enough to pay for two persons at Radcliffe—Helen and Anne. Without her beloved teacher to be her eyes and ears, Helen could not even hope to go to college.

42   Old friends stepped in to help. Mark Twain, Alexander Graham Bell, and others raised money to pay for college. But there were even greater problems.

43   For the first time in her life, Helen would be going to a normal school. She would be sitting in classes with girls who could see and hear. How would she be able to hear the teacher's lectures? How could she see what was written on the chalkboard? How could she take notes, read textbooks, do homework, or write examinations? There was only one way—through Anne Sullivan.

Helen Keller (left) with Anne Sullivan.

44   Her teacher had never gone to college. Yet hour after hour, she would have to spell out into Helen's hand, quickly and correctly, lectures on subjects she herself did not understand. Evening after evening, she would have to "read" into Helen's palm from the textbooks.

45   Anne's eyes were weak. Her sight was never clear or strong. For four years, she strained her eyes to help Helen through college. During these difficult years, Helen somehow found the time to write *The Story of My Life*, her first book. In it, she told the story of how Anne Sullivan had led her from a sad and lonely life to one that was happy and full. Anne helped with the book, but the writing itself was Helen's own.

46   In 1904, Helen Keller was graduated from Radcliffe with honors. She completed her studies in the usual four years. She proved to the world—and to herself—that a blind and deaf person can do as well in college as anybody else.

Finding the Main Idea

5. The main idea of paragraph 36 appears in sentence:
   (*a*) 1   (*b*) 2   (*c*) 3   (*d*) 4

6. The main idea of paragraphs 40–46 concerns:
   (*a*) Helen's growing fame
   (*b*) her well-known friends
   (*c*) the writing of her first book
   (*d*) her college education

Part IV

47   **After her graduation** from Radcliffe, Helen began her own lifework. She raised money to help persons who were blind or deaf. Starting in Massachusetts, she worked for the blind or deaf in many states. Years later, she helped establish the American Foundation for the Blind.

48   To raise more money, Helen and Anne decided to go on a lecture tour. In 1913, Helen stood for the first time on a public stage in Montclair, New Jersey. She could not see the audience or tell whether her voice was too high or too low, too loud or too soft. She felt terribly alone and helpless. When she finished speaking for the blind, she felt the stage floor shake under her feet. It was from the long, loud clapping of the audience.

49   About this time, a young woman named Polly Thompson joined them. She quickly learned the hand alphabet. Both Helen and Anne liked this clever and lively person. She became Helen's secretary.

50   The three women were always busy. Helen gave four or five lectures a week. After each lecture, Polly led her around the lecture room, where Helen collected money for the blind in a basket.

51   With Polly and Anne, Helen traveled around the country in vaudeville shows. Some people wondered how she could "lower herself" to appear in vaudeville shows. These shows generally included singers, dancers, comics, magicians, and trained animals. But Helen knew what she was doing. She used the money that she made from vaudeville to help other blind or deaf people.

52   In the 1930s, Anne began to feel the strain of all these busy years. Her health failed. Worst of all, her eyesight gave out. Years and years of reading for Helen had been too much of a strain on her eyes. In the end, she became completely blind.

53   Anne Sullivan died in 1936. This was surely the worst moment in Helen's life. She felt as if she had lost her "other self." However, her teacher had done her work well. She had taught Helen to be brave and to overcome great hardships. Now Helen knew that she must go on without her teacher.

54   With Polly to help her, Helen traveled widely in Europe. Wherever she went, she lectured and raised money for the blind. She even went as far away as Japan. Her work in that country was of great help in setting up schools and libraries for the blind.

55   During World War Two, Helen visited over 70 hospitals. She comforted the many soldiers and sailors blinded in battle. The example of her own life and success brought hope to these men.

56   After the war, Polly and she took up their travels again. The war had left blind people in many countries. It had also destroyed schools and libraries for the blind. In Europe, Africa, South America, and the Far East, Helen once again lectured and raised money for the blind.

57   When Polly died in 1959, Helen was an old woman. She lived in a house built especially for her in Westport, Connecticut. Many good friends there helped her and kept her company.

58   In 1968, Helen Keller died at the age of 88. People all over the world praised her long and useful life. Only Helen knew how great a part of her life Anne Sullivan had been. In *The Story of My Life*, Helen wrote:

My teacher is so near to me that I scarcely think of myself apart from her. All the best of me belongs to her—there is not a talent or a hope or a joy in me that has not been awakened by her loving touch.

59   In 1980, the Post Office issued a stamp showing Helen Keller with Anne Sullivan. The United States

Congress set aside her birthday—June 27—as Helen Keller Day. All over the world, organizations and people who knew her honored the birth, 100 years before, of the woman who brought help and hope to the blind and the blind-deaf.

Working with Words

7. When things look *blurred* (paragraph 5), they appear:
(*a*) broken   (*b*) distant   (*c*) unclear   (*d*) sharp

8. A *stubborn* (paragraph 15) child will generally:
(*a*) want his or her own way   (*b*) obey others
(*c*) learn quickly   (*d*) become ill

9. Use the following words to complete the sentences below.
> inventor (paragraph 39)
> inventive
> invent
> invention

a. Dr. Alexander Graham Bell was a famous _____ .
b. His best-known _____ is the telephone.
c. He was able to _____ the telephone because of his lifelong interest in hearing and deafness.
d. Only a truly _____ person could have created such a useful device.

10. The word *destroyed* (paragraph 56) most nearly means:
(*a*) created   (*b*) wrecked   (*c*) left   (*d*) described

EXERCISES

Putting Events in Sequence

A.   Write the letters of each set of events in the order in which the events happened in Helen Keller's and Anne Sullivan's lives. For example, would you answer #1 by writing *a-b* or *b-a*? If you need help, look back at the story.

1. *a.* Anne Sullivan becomes Helen Keller's teacher.
   b. Helen learns to obey.

2. *a.* Helen learns to speak using her own voice.
   b. Helen begins to learn language.

3. *a.* Helen lectures in public for the first time.
   b. With Anne to help her, Helen goes to college.

4. *a.* Polly Thompson becomes Helen's secretary.
   b. Anne Sullivan dies.

5. *a.* Polly dies.
   b. Helen travels to many other countries to work for the deaf and blind.

Making Inferences

   B.   Use what you have read about Anne Sullivan and Helen Keller to infer, or figure out, the correct choice.

1. The key for Helen to learn to use language was:
   (*a*) being willing to obey
   (*b*) learning to use the hand alphabet
   (*c*) understanding that words stand for things
   (*d*) learning enough words

2. Besides being deaf and blind, Helen was evidently:
   (*a*) musically gifted   (*b*) very intelligent
   (*c*) mentally retarded   (*d*) uninterested in learning

3. You could infer that people liked Helen for her:
   (*a*) sense of humor (*b*) pretty face (*c*) kindness and generosity (*d*) courage and cheerfulness

4. In addition to teaching Helen to use language, Anne also served her as a model for:
   (*a*) helping others   (*b*) lecturing in public
   (*c*) writing books   (*d*) making a living

Understanding Cause and Effect

C. Write the letter of the correct choice.

1. As a result of childhood illness, Anne Sullivan had been:
   (*a*) deaf   (*b*) blind
   (*c*) both deaf and blind   (*d*) unable to speak

2. Being blind and deaf actually helped Helen learn more quickly because:
   (*a*) people felt sorry for her
   (*b*) books in Braille are better written than printed books
   (*c*) the outside world couldn't distract her from learning
   (*d*) it made her more intelligent than other children her age

3. Helen needed to get more money for college because:
   (*a*) she had no money of her own
   (*b*) she had to pay for Anne's attendance, too
   (*c*) she wished to make a gift to Radcliffe
   (*d*) she wanted to repay Mark Twain and Alexander Graham Bell

4. The U.S. Post Office issued a stamp bearing a picture of Helen and Anne because it wanted to:
   (*a*) inspire deaf and blind people
   (*b*) sell more stamps
   (*c*) celebrate Helen's birthday
   (*d*) honor the two women

Separating Fact from Opinion

D. Tell which is a *fact* and which is an *opinion*.

1. As a small child, Helen Keller could not see, hear, or speak.

2. Only Anne Sullivan could have taught Helen to understand language.

3. Helen outlived both Anne Sullivan and Polly Thompson.

4. Despite her handicaps, Helen traveled all over the world.

Choosing the Best Title

E. Write the best title for the story of Helen Keller and Anne Sullivan.

1. Reading in Braille
2. Taming a Wild Girl
3. Organizations for the Handicapped
4. Two Women Work Miracles

Speaking, Listening, and Writing

F. Be prepared to talk briefly about one of the following topics by writing some notes to yourself. (You may wish to make up a name for the real person you choose to tell about.)

1. Tell about the best teacher you ever had. What made this teacher so good?
2. Tell about someone you know or know about who learned to do something very difficult.

G. Write a paragraph or more about one of the following topics.

1. How did Helen Keller help others as she grew older?
2. Helen Keller was lucky to have such a good teacher. What made Anne Sullivan a good teacher? Write your answer in the form of a letter from Helen to Anne.
3. Tell about how you learned to do something that was very difficult. How did you feel about it?